BAD DATES

BAD DATES

Celebrities
(and Other Talented Types)
Reveal Their Worst Nights Out

by Carole Markin

A Citadel Press Book
Published by Carol Publishing Group

A Citadel Press Book
Published by Carol Publishing Group

Editorial Offices
600 Madison Avenue
New York, NY 10022

Sales & Distribution Offices
120 Enterprise Avenue
Secaucus, NJ 07094

In Canada: Musson Book Company
A division of General Publishing Co. Limited
Don Mills, Ontario

Manufactured in the United States of America

Library of Congress Cataloging-in-Publication Data

Markin, Carole.
    Bad dates : celebrities (and other talented types) reveal
their worst nights out / by Carole Markin.
        p. cm.
    "A Citadel Press book."
    ISBN 0-8065-1158-3
    1. Celebrities--United States--Biography. 2. Embarrassing
or uncomfortable moments on dates--personal experiences.
I. Title. II: Celebrities reveal their worst nights out.
1990 [B]

Dedicated to my parents
whose first date was so bad
it's amazing they ever produced me

Introduction

Ever since I was thirteen years old, people have tried to fix me up on dates. As a result, I've had a lot of bad ones. This is not to say that I was a masochist or desperate; I was merely open-minded and figured the worst thing that could happen was that I'd come back with a good story.

For years I entertained my friends with tales of romantic woe. During one particularly ridiculous period of rotten luck and bizarre coincidences, a male friend of mine suggested I write a book about my encounters. I thanked him for his faith in me as a fascinating subject, but suggested that the general public might be slightly more interested in the romantic catastrophes of the rich and famous.

Having never written a book before, I embarked upon the process as an independent filmmaker would—convinced that I could get it done through my resourcefulness, persistence and acquired ability to make cold telephone calls. There was, however, one minor problem. I was scared to talk to famous people. Falling back on the practice I learned at college—you can always talk your way around the word "no"—I proceeded to write thousands of letters, make thousands of phone calls, crash parties, accost people in restaurants, beg favors, sneak onto movie sets, and get thrown out of baseball dugouts.

What I collected on this odyssey was a series of honest and on-the-record, first-person accounts based primarily on conversations with top people in a variety of fields: athletes, entertainers, poets, painters, politicians and business executives. The stories range from the innocent to the outrageous, from the hilarious to the tender, even the kinky. In an era when media consultants groom people's grocery lists, the candor of the contributions was both refreshing and rewarding.

When I began, I had three hunches: that intense careers color all aspects of personal lives, including bad dates; that the definition of "bad" is widely divergent; and that when it comes to dating, all people experience similar emotions. Sure enough, the musicians stumbled into trouble while on tour, while the feminist ran up against a chauvinist. Whereas the desire for a good date was indeed universal, the notion of bad included wrong name, wrong person, false teeth and tattoos; sharp tongues and dull knives; lost love and lost lunch. On the emotional front, I discovered that even people who have complete control of their professional lives can have moments when they are vulnerable.

I thank the participants for their time, tales, and courage to speak frankly, and hope that next time Ronald Reagan, Meryl Streep and Axl Rose will return my calls.

Carole Markin

Acknowledgments

You cannot produce a book like *Bad Dates*, with its myriad of negotiations and details, by yourself. First I would like to thank publisher Steven Schragis and my editor Liza Wachter for taking a risk with me and for putting the full resources of Carol Publishing Group behind this very time-consuming project. Liza, in particular, deserves special praise for her complete and tireless commitment to making this book the best that it could be.

I owe immense gratitude to my hardworking and underpaid lawyer, Evan Cohen, and to my agent, Michael Siegel. In addition, I am appreciative of the work and resources provided by the staffs of their respective offices, Cohen & Luckenbacher and H. N. Swanson.

I also thank the staff of Independent Feature Project/West, including, but not limited to, Randy Skupinsky, Russell Martin, Sau-Wah Tsang, Ralph Rugoff, Janet Smith, Patrick Scott, for putting up with the extra burden I imposed on the office. As for the board of directors of Independent Feature Project/West, I greatly appreciate the support and resources of its members, especially Jeanne Lucas, Susan Lynch, Doug Edwards, Wil Hobbs, Barbara Boyle, Peter Broderick, Carolyn Pfeiffer, Anne Kimmel, Victoria Wozniak, Ed Landler, Howard Rodman, David Burton Morris, John Esaki, Gwen Field, Jane Alsobrook, Ira Deutchman, Bonni Lee, Midge Sanford, and Peter Elson.

For photographs, I recognize and appreciate the generosity of the Los Angeles Lakers, the NBA, the Los Angeles Raiders, Al LoCasle, the Baltimore Colts, the St. Louis Cardinals, Cleveland Public Library, Associated Press, the St. Louis Post Disptach, ABC, NBC, Yorum Globus, Peter Murray, Howard Mandelbaum, Chip Stone, Fran Kuntz, William Klein, Warner Brothers, Paramount, New Line Cinema, and the host of photographers whose work is credited in the book.

One day I will be able to repay my debt to my assorted "in-house counsels", including Steve Berman, Doug Brotherton, Dan Freeman, James Greenberg, Maureen Crowe, Chris Monger, David Himmelfarb, Alan Holleb, Mel Markon, Jody Cukier, Jill Kearney, Chris Ruppenthal, Martin Cohen, Larry Olney, Lois Markin, Howard Markin, Sophie Markin, Bob Markin, Rose Markin, and other members of my extended family.

I thank the following people for opening doors, providing addresses, spotting celebrities on street corners and performing other ridiculous tasks that sometimes required some persuasion: Jon S. Denny, Suzan Bymel, Evelyn O'Neill, David Lewis, Danica Kombol, Patti Gilbert, Randal Michaelson, Nancye Ferguson, Alana Rothstein, Michael Lally, Eve Brandstein, Steve Feigenbaum, Wil Akers, Bobby Rock, Boyce Harmon, David Claussin, Don Dortch, Joanna Samuels, Pat Foulkrod, Jim Katz, Peter McCarthy, Catherine Hardwicke, Lauren Cardillo, Michael Kurcfeld, Scott Fields, Michael Nolin, Jill Alman, Ned Tanen, Lynn McKissick, Amy Atkins, Susan Ninenger, Kate Ninenger, Debby Trutnick, Hope Wilder, Loree Rodkin, Marco Williams, Chris Gerolmo, Peter Lang, Nina Reznick, Ed Saxon, Mona Simpson, Alan Frank, Benjamin Krepak, Steve McCue, Vikram Jayanti, Jacek Laskus, Janet Sternberg, Grant Morris, David Blyth, Tom Schiller, Lisa Sawahata, Mary Lou, H. N. Swanson, Karen Rubin, Mel Graybar, Richard Sherman, Jacki Apple, Barry White, Bill Brezski, Loren Pullman, Chris Giodono, Francine Lipsman, Eddie Michaels, Erin, Elon Dershowitz, Carol Stuart, Kathy Pinkert, Deac Rossell, Sue Patricola, Claudia Kunin, Pearl Beach, Justin Kaplan, Phillip Epstein, and Ben Petrone. If I forgot you, please forgive me.

My assistants Julia Jackson, Nancy Harris, Maureen O'Sullivan, Lori Fontanes, Beth Jasper, and Nicole Dillenberg deserve a tremendous round of applause for their efforts.

Finally, a heartfelt special thanks goes to Ann Siegel for her invaluable assistance and perfect touch with key people.

I could go on, but we need the space for the text.

Thanks, thanks, thanks.

Carole Markin

Contents

BAD DATES

Kareem Abdul-Jabbar

The leading scorer in NBA history, legendary center Kareem Abdul-Jabbar completed his twentieth pro season and embarked on a new career in the entertainment business as both an actor and a producer. In addition, Kareem owns a jazz record label.

I never had much success with the ladies. I was always the most retiring guy in the crowd, last to be noticed by the girls looking for a ringleader or a Romeo. I was always hoping for some young lady to read my silence as sensitivity and have enough of her own to let me know she was open to romance. I was a dreamer. Going to an all-boys Catholic high school where they as much as checked your palms for hair also didn't help. Plus, generally hanging around with older guys, I was always the least experienced, the most impressionable.

And those guys would lie something fierce. The dudes that were doing all the talking—Vino, Victor, and Kelly—they'd lie about all kinds of shit. Vino, that was his specialty. He'd come back and tell stories about orgies he had been to over here and wild parties he'd gone to over there. Like, "Oh, yeah, and there were these babes from Brooklyn, and they took us to this place like you've never seen, man, and there was us and these six chicks and..." Or, "So we left this pad in the projects, man. And we was grabbin' at each other and it got to where we just couldn't wait so...I got some in

3

the stairwell." That's how it would always end up: he got laid. But when we were at parties with Vino, nothing ever seemed to happen, except for him getting drunk and acting crazy.

But I believed these guys; I believed most of what people told me. They were running all over town sampling the vineyards, and I was woefully alone.

And things never quite went my way. There was a girl who lived on Riverside Drive and 156th Street, Cheri Benoit, who I really liked and who was starting to return the favor. She was a year younger than I was, and she'd come up, and we'd sit around and kiss on the couch when my parents weren't home. When they were, I'd get antsy and say, "We gotta get out of here"; so we'd go downstairs, and it would be thirty degrees outside, and I'd sit out there on the bench with her all bundled up.

One day we were walking together, and Cheri said, "Come on, let's run down the hill." She took off, and I was trailing after her in my best athlete's lope when, one sneaker over another, I tripped and sprawled forward like an oaf. I took two steps while pitching out of control, trying desperately to maintain my balance, but the hill only got steeper and I finally just went down. My knees skinned against the pavement, tearing huge holes in my pants as I tried to break my fall. I lay there, stunned. After enduring and then outgrowing all my on-court humiliations, I had to be a hopeless clod in front of the first nice girl who lets me touch her. Cheri ran back, saying "Gee, can I help you?" I pulled myself up, palms scraped, these great big holes at least six inches across in my pants, blood coming out of my knees. Why me? We ended up going to her house; she stung me with a whole lot of iodine, and I hobbled home.

Not long afterwards, Kelly and I were discussing the various assets of the neighborhood ladies. Kelly was into music; we'd go down to the Village Vanguard and hear some jazz together, and he was reasonably well-read with an agile mind. He was a good friend if you got him alone, but he did go on about getting the job done. He didn't know I liked Cheri; I was always very careful not to let anyone in on who I was seeing. Didn't want a lot of loose talk.

"Man, I had Cheri up there the other day," he told me confidentially, "and I almost got something." I thought, Oh, no. But I didn't let on as Kelly gave me the details.

I didn't talk to Cheri for six months. I figured Kelly was telling the truth, and since he was good-looking and a proven charmer, she was locked up. Besides, the whole thing was now somehow tainted. I kind of missed Cheri, but I figured there was nothing I could do.

Finally, I ran into her. She had been confused, then angry, then sad, wondering what ever happened to me. Though she was a year younger than I, I had never thought of her as vulnerable, only either uncaring or taken.

"But you and Kelly..." "You know, I talked to Kelly," she said with a sixteen-year-old's dignity, "but that's it." Still, at that age hurt runs real deep, and things were not really right between us for a long time.

Jimmy Aleck

Jimmy Aleck is an "everyday kind of guy" who also happens to be a rising young comedian. He has appeared regularly on *The Tonight Show starring Johnny Carson, Late Night with David Letterman*, and *The Arsenio Hall Show*, and has toured with stars such as Diana Ross, Tom Jones, Tina Turner and Willie Nelson.

For some unknown reason, when I was 16 I could buy beer.

I could buy it as long as I was wearing... 'My Outfit'—the same jacket, the same hat, the same sunglasses. I would always carry 'My Outfit' with me in the car, just in case my buddies and I wanted anything.

One Thanksgiving I was at the parents' house of this girl I was dating, having Thanksgiving dinner, and my buddies pull up. Knock! Knock! Knock! "Hey, Jimmy here?" "He's here." her mother cried. "Your friends are out there, Jimmy," she says to me. I said, "Ohhh?" (Like what are they doing here?)

I go to the door and my two buddies say, "We'd like some beer. Buy us some. Get your outfit." "I'm not buying you guys beer. It's

Thanksgiving, Thanksgiving dinner." They go, "If you don't buy us beer, we can cause some problems... You don't wanta get us upset, DO YOU?"

I *knew* what they would do. They would moon the house or honk the horn or yell dirty words or something. They *would* do that, my friends.

Like once, we were out on a triple date to the drive-in, and we weren't getting along too well with the girls we had gone out with, so, when the three girls went to the bathroom, my buddies moved the car. The girls didn't think it was too funny. "Well, you didn't see your faces when you came out the bathroom. Now *that* was funny! Ha Ha ha." These guys were that rude!

That's why, when I went back to the table after talking to the guys, I said to my date, "Listen, I have to go for about half an hour." She got so upset. "How could you leave my parents' dinner?" I said, "Listen, it is for the better, believe me. If I don't go, you'll regret it. *Believe* me." "I don't believe you." "Ask your brothers. *They*'ll understand. *They*'ll tell you. If your buddies ask, you had BETTER go!" And I left.

I came back about *two hours* later, in the middle of Thanksgiving dinner. I walked in and said to the family, "I just had to go somewhere with my friends." Some story. My date scowled at me, her older brothers nodded, and then the father said, "Jimmy, what's wrong with your eyes?" I said, "Oh, my contact lenses are probably bothering me. Do you mind if I go to the bathroom before I sit down?"

I got to the bathroom and I looked in the mirror, and I saw I had my glasses on. So I figured the father knew I'd had a little something while I was out. But he didn't say anything. Neither did his daughter.

After dinner she was even more upset. "Don't be upset." I said, "Your father is cool. Look how he acts when we're down in the den watching TV and kissing and he wants some ice cream. He goes, 'Okay, well Rose, I think I'm going to go down to the den now and get some ice cream! I'm going down there, WHERE JIMMY AND LYNN ARE, and I'm going to get some ICE CREAM! You want any *ICE CREAM*!!!????' He understands that. He'll understand this."

I tried everything to get her out of that mood. Even rubbing her stomach. Usually that gets the girls to go AHHH—their arms fall by their side, like some kind of alligator. Not this girl.

I'm sure she thought I was a jerk. When you're sixteen, you really are.

Steve Allen

Multitalented Steve Allen created *The Tonight Show*; authored thirty-two books; starred on Broadway and in motion pictures; wrote over 4,000 songs; wrote scores for several musicals for Broadway and TV; made over forty record albums; starred in the acclaimed NBC series *The Steve Allen Comedy Hour*, and created, wrote, and hosted the Emmy-winning PBS series *Meeting of the Minds*.

When she stepped out of the rickety elevator and walked toward me, eyebrows raised pleadingly, I looked at her and something inside me said "Oh," softly. It was the sort of "oh" that children at boarding school speak on Sundays when they are told that no one is coming to visit them, the sort of "oh" that a student breathes when he is informed that he has failed an examination, the sort of "oh" to which a man gives voice when told he is no longer needed at his office.

"You haven't changed," I said, lying as I looked at her plain seventeen-year-old face and then quickly, almost accidentally, down at the gawky body in the severe drab green cloth coat and the long feet in shoes with depressingly low heels.

Later that night, riding home alone in the streetcar, I remembered the shoes. If only she had not worn them. Her face certainly wasn't the most unattractive I have ever seen and her body wasn't too heavy, but the shoes had colored her entire personality in an instant. They looked like the shoes that foreign maids or tired, elderly women wore and so unlike the shoes I had vaguely associated with my longed-for, dreamed-about Woman.

"I still can't get over your remembering me," she said as we walked along under the elevated on Sixty-third Street.

"Well," I said, "it was just one of those things. I didn't know a lot of kids at school when I was twelve because, you know, I was new and all, and I guess you were about the only girl that paid attention to me. And then, too, I remember that you were very pretty."

"My gosh," she said.

"I don't mean you're not now," I said awkwardly, "but I just mean that I remember how you looked. You had long, long hair and you laughed all the time."

"Did I?"

We turned south at the corner of Sixty-third and Stoney Island Avenue and began walking along the edge of the park, huddling slightly closer now as we leaned into the gusty wind together.

Ah, what a creature she had been the moment before she appeared in that dingy lobby of the rundown apartment hotel. Long brown hair, the hair I remembered having seen blowing and tossing in the fresh winds of that almost forgotten spring as she had run skittering and giggling about in the schoolyard, her brown eyes flashing, her face glowing with an open, impish smile. This image I had combined with my who-knows-how-created ideal, merged with faces seen in dreams, faces seen on movie screens (I had confidently expected to see a certain wry Carole Lombardish sophistication superimposed onto the face of Kathryn Kelly—with just a suggestion of Claudette Colbert—step out of the elevator).

But here I was, walking in the cold October darkness with a poor, virginal, vapid creature who seemed very like a stranger.

"A penny for your thoughts," Kathryn said.

"I'm sorry," I said, "I guess my mind was a million miles away. You want to see a movie?"

We walked on silently. I experimented with my emotions, trying to recapture my earlier mood, trying to convince myself that with more lipstick and high heels Kathryn might still be considered attractive.

There was something unusual about the feeling she aroused in me; my pity for her was so strong that it quite evaporated my usual embarrassment at being with a girl. The presence of a pretty, vivacious girl was usually enough to make me blissfully bumbling, almost dopily shy. But now I felt strangely mature and wise.

We walked into the Tivoli and sat down near the front of the theater. The movie was *Rhythm on the Range* and as we went in Bing Crosby was singing "Empty Saddles." Sitting in the darkness, smelling her Lifebouy-and-powder scent, feeling the heat of her body, I was able after half an hour or so to begin idealizing her features once again, altering the reality of her just enough so that in time it seemed that a provocative and interesting feminine creature was sitting next to me after all. Within an hour I had gotten up enough nerve to slip my left arm around the back of her chair and rest it, as if accidentally, on her shoulders.

Observing that she did not withdraw at this modest liberty, I was emboldened to, oh so gradually, work the arm completely off the back of the seat and quite definitely around her in a loose sort of embrace. At this she turned to me for a moment and smiled. I was too embarrassed to look directly into her eyes at such close quarters, but did lean a bit closer to her.

This was as far as physical matters progressed. When the picture was over I avoided looking at her directly 'til we were on the streetcar going home.

We walked in silence back to the apartment hotel where I had picked her up. Its lobby looked dingier than ever.

"Well," I said, shaking her hand awkwardly, noting that she wore no nail polish, "it's been a lot of fun. I hope to see you again."

"That would be nice." There was a leaden pause.

"Well, I guess you have to be running upstairs."

"Yes," she said, "have to get my beauty sleep."

"Yeah. Well, I'll be seein' ya." "So long."

Outside I turned my coat collar and walked along Sixty-third Street, feeling angry and depressed.

On the streetcar going back to my own neighborhood I sat with half-closed eyes, rocking sleepily with the motion of the car. By the time I had reached my stop I had contrived to make Kathryn seem prettier in my mind than she had actually been. When I got off the streetcar I was thinking about her knees—or somebody's knees.

Lyle Alzado

Lyle Alzado was an All-Pro defensive end for the Denver Broncos. Currently a game analyst for NBC sports, he has also appeared on national commercials and talk shows. As an actor, his TV and film credits include: "Amazing Stories," "Riptide," and the features, *The Destroyer* and *Who's Harry Crumb?*

"Is she pretty?"

"She's great, you're gonna love her."

"Are you sure?"

"She's great, you're gonna love her."

"I don't like blind dates."

"She's great, you're gonna love her."

I didn't love her when she opened the door. She scared me half to death. I mean, this girl was as big as me! She must have weighed 300 pounds.

All I could think of was, where's my teammate? I'm gonna chase him around the neighborhood for this one. But I didn't want to be rude to her because she was a friend of his girlfriend, so I said, "Let's talk for a few minutes in your place." What I really needed was some time to think of somewhere to take this girl for dinner where none of my friends would see us.

A funny thing happened, though. Once I talked to her, I realized she was really a wonderful person. I said to myself, I don't care if they're all used to seeing me with models or great-looking girls in the movie business, I'm gonna take her where I normally go. So we went to Studio 54 and to Chelsea's and a bunch of places like that and had a great time.

While we danced she kept telling me, "I'm the best thing that'll ever happen to you. I'm the best thing." She might have been, but at twenty two I couldn't see it. So when she tried to feel me up, I said, "Look, I'm not that kind of guy."

Only kidding. I kissed her goodnight and we became good friends for a very long time. She turned out to be one of the most wonderful people I have ever met.

Kathy Arendsen

*Kathy Arendsen talks
with her team on the mound*

Three-time Amateur Softball Association Player of the Year, Kathy Arendsen gained national attention when she struck out slugger Reggie Jackson on ABC's *Wide World of Sports.* Now head softball coach at Eastern Illinois University, she continues to rank as one of the top pitchers in the world.

First of all, you have to understand, I'm six foot two, so I'm not just your average female. I'm from a Dutch family, and the Dutch tend to run tall: my father is 6'5", my brother is 6'6", my mom is 5'9", my sister is the runt at 5'7". I have a grandmother who's taller than I am and at least ten cousins who are my height or taller. In fact, where I grew up, on our high school girls' basketball team, our center was 6'5", our power forward was 6'3". I was the small forward at 6'2" so I never viewed myself as being tall or different. Only when other people react, that's when I know I'm tall.

I never wear real high heels. The highest heels I would wear (even with a skirt) are about an inch, inch and a half. Which was what I was wearing the night of my blind date.

My date arrives. I open the door. I wanted to go immediately and put flats on. The guy was 5'5". He probably wished he had elevator shoes. Instead, he said, "Do you play basketball or something?"

"Yeah. I play. I guess, if my friend had told you that, you might have had a clue I'd be this tall."

"You must be pretty good."

"I'm all right. But I'm a better softball pitcher."

We both laughed and went out to his car.

The car. That was another story. It was a sea-green Dodge with a bench seat, so if he adjusts his seat, I'm adjusted as well. I mean, we were stuck with my legs wedged under my chin. The poor man had to drive.

The restaurant. There's really no problem when you're sitting down and eating. Not surprisingly, I was the tallest woman he had ever dated. I told him I tended to go out with guys who were an inch or two inches shorter than me. But I pointed out that the real problem came when people didn't realize I was a girl.

I have short curly hair, and when I'm not dressed in a dress, anything can happen. Like the time a saleslady chased me into the bathroom crying, "Excuse me, SIR. *This* is the *ladies room!*" I turned to her and said, "I *know.*" She was mighty embarrassed. He thought that was funny.

The local tavern. Everything was okay with the fast songs. Of course, everybody was looking at us: we were a very odd pair.

A slow song came up. We started to move into position. He hesitated a bit. I said, "What the hell, come on, I don't care if your head is in my chest."

The goodnight kiss. We also passed on that. I would have had to get down on my hands and knees, practically, or arrange to have him stand on something. Before this, I really wasn't aware of the problems that shorter people have to deal with.

The result. We ended up being good friends. Still, I'd have to say, he was a great sport.

Steven Arnold

Surrealist Artist Steven Arnold is a photographer, filmmaker, ballet choreographer, and set and costume designer. His work is in the permanent archives of institutions such as the Museum of Modern Art, New York City, Cinemathéque Français, Paris, and the Whitney Museum of Art. His photos have appeared in major magazines from *Vogue* to *Photo Japan*.

Salvador Dali and his wife, Gala, had a very European marriage. She was usually with pretty, young boys, blonds, and he was usually with transvestites. It was always like that, in Spain, in New York, wherever. They'd all go out to restaurants together and she would sit with her date and he would sit with his all evening.

This particular night, Gala had been running her fingers through my hair a lot and was being very nice to me. I had shoulder-length blond hair at the time, and was their house guest in Spain while I helped Dali prepare for the 1976 opening of the Salvador Dali Museum. As might be expected, Dali asked me if I would be Gala's date for the following evening.

I'd always been a little afraid of Gala. She was extremely sharp and outspoken and a little bit scary, although elegant at the same time. Beautifully dressed, beautifully jeweled, beautifully coiffed, always, always, always. Even in the summer.

She had a castle sixty miles away from Dali's castle, where she lived most of the time. They had separate staffs. Her staff wore powder-blue uniforms copied after Nesbit Cafeteria in New York City, with funny little hats, and his servants wore pink uniforms in the same style. They both had Cadillac limousines, black ones, with red upholstery, and they both had chauffeurs.

Dali couldn't go to Gala's castle unless he received a written invitation, which he seldom did. Nevertheless, he was madly in love with her. They'd talk on the phone every day for hours and would always hold hands in public. It was so strange. She was stranger than he was, in a lot of ways... which is certainly hard to get.

So Dali asked me if I would be Gala's date, and I said, "Sure."

I dressed carefully in an all-white suit with a Pace-Cellini brooch at the top of my necktie. We met at the Ritz in Barcelona for dinner. Dali was there, too, with a famous transsexual, who's a woman, but who was originally a man, I think. Anyway, very beautiful and very brilliant.

Gala immediately started pulling my hair, and as the evening progressed, she pulled harder and harder. Then, at one particularly painful moment, she whispered, "After dinner, I'm going to take you in my limousine and we're going to drive to my castle and I'm going to torture you slowly."

I had heard rumors that she was into bondage. She liked to dress boys up as girls in women's underwear and makeup and play with them for hours like a cat. I don't think she ever really hurt anybody, but I was getting a bit concerned, because she was pulling on my hair until it hurt, and also pinching me sharply in the ribs and on my legs.

I looked over to Dali for help. He completely ignored me. I wasn't with him anymore, I was with HER. I had joined HER camp.

Finally, we walked out to her limousine and I said, "Look, I don't think I'll go. I have to get up early tomorrow and take some photographs."

She was furious. She slammed the limousine door, spat at me out the window, drove off in a cloud of dust, and never spoke to me again. Never looked me in the eye. Just turned her head.

I regret the decision to this day. I wish I'd gone just to see what she would have put me through and to see the inside of her castle. The pictures of it are just unbelievable! All the ceilings were muraled by Dali, the furniture is Art Nuevo and Baroque, and it's filled with stuffed animals, which Gala would talk to and play with, like a child.

When the limousine dust settled, I went back to Dali's camp, and now he was my friend. He held my hand the rest of the evening and whispered endearments in my ear in French, Spanish and several other languages, because he was in the habit of deliberately confusing people.

In a way, I don't regret the decision. Gala might have kept me in her castle for days. And then Dali and I would never have become very close. I guess you might say, I failed her loyalty test, but I passed his.

Isaac Asimov

One of the world's most prolific writers of science fiction, Isaac Asimov has also covered topics ranging from biochemistry to limericks in over 330 books.

ALEX GOTFRYD

I didn't have many dates, because I married at twenty-two, after a busy youth in which I had no time for girls. When my first marriage broke up, I quickly arranged for a second marriage. So I've had practically no bachelor life.

What dates I did have were all interesting, all fun. After all, I'm the one that supplies the interest and the fun and all I ask of a girl is that she listen and, at the right moments, laugh. Under those circumstances, how can they be bad? For me, anyway?

Catherine Bach

Catherine Bach is best known as the vehicle-wise beauty on *Dukes of Hazzard*. Her feature film credits include: *Cannonball II, Thunderbolt & Lightfoot,* and *The Widow.*

I was about, oh, god, eleven years old and I was invited on a trip, a vacation, up to a lake, with my best girlfriend's family. She was a little older than me, maybe thirteen, so she had a little more of a body. She was my favorite girlfriend in the whole world and we were both just starting to get a little boy crazy.

The first night at the lake, we went to a dance and we saw all these beautiful men, who were probably all of fourteen or fifteen years old. To us, they seemed like "really men." It was wonderful! Every boy was my dream man. I think that is the way it is when you are young. *Now* my dream man is tall, dark, handsome (and definitely going off the market), but *then*, it was anything that was a boy, I think.

My girlfriend and I were really interested in these two darling boys, who were friends. They both had great tans, and they both had brown hair with streaks in it, and they both were fifteen. We all had a great time at the dance and said we would meet them at the beach the next day.

I really wanted to look good in my bathing suit. But we had lied about our age and had told them we were fifteen, and I wasn't even wearing a... you know, lingerie at the time, so I said to my girlfriend, "I can't go out there looking like this."

She said, "You're right."

My girlfriend had a polka-dot bikini just like "the itsy, bitsy, teeny, weeny" one in the song. She gave it to me and I stuffed it with her mother's nylons. Single nylons. Her mother was a "single nylon woman." (Nobody was wearing panty hose at the time.) I had one or two nylons in each of my boobs and I *knew* I was lookin' "pretttty goooood."

We met the boys on the beach, we went for a swim, and it was definitely love.

I got out of the water. It was a beautiful, hot day. These two guys were standing over us looking beautiful too. I was sitting there with my legs outstretched and my arms behind me, with my hair wet and a big smile on my face, going, "I love you. I want to be with you for the rest of my life," in my mind. And I'm thinking, "Yeah, boy. I got the body. I don't blame them for looking at my body." Then, I saw their eyes looking at me, but they weren't looking at my body...

They were staring at this *nylon foot*—wet, sopping, dripping down my stomach. It was down to my belly button! Everybody was wearing cinnamon tan and suntan cinnamon nylons at the time, with dark spots in the heel and toe, so it was *really* noticeable.

My date said, "What's that?" I jumped, "Oh, nothing."

I have to say I didn't know what to do. I mean, I was really a little kid! Men were a new experience; it wasn't the time of "Let's laugh and be cool about this and share."

I didn't know if I should act like the nylon foot was the lining of the bathing suit or what. It didn't look like lining; it looked like a cinnamon foot coming out of my top! (Now I have a lot of sympathy for all these guys walking around with socks in their shorts, that's all I have got to say!)

And my girlfriend, oh, she was dying. She turned beet red. The guys figured, if I had 'em, she probably had 'em. Which she did. Yeah, she was definitely padded for the occasion.

What I finally did was, I slowly laid down on the beach and started putting tanning oil on my body. And as my hand spread the oil, I tried to surreptitiously tuck the foot back into the suit and pretend like nobody saw it. Because I was completely mortified. I didn't know what I was going to do with the rest of my life.

That was it for boys. From then on, I decided to concentrate on my water skiing...and stuff my bathing suit with falsies.

Paul Bartel

Film director/writer/producer/actor Paul Bartel feels that if his material doesn't offend, it isn't working. Best known for his mischevious comedies *Eating Raoul* and *Scenes from a Class Struggle in Beverly Hills*, Paul also is a jury member of many international film festivals.

According to my observation, "bad dates" are generally the business of adolescence. But I live in a town (Hollywood) and work in a business (the movies) where the inconveniences of youth are often foisted on the mature. So, when the girl I'll call "Basha" barged briefly into my life, I probably should have been prepared.

Basha was a minor actress from an Eastern European country, let's call it "Hungary." She was the friend of a good friend of mine, Gregor Pirelli, an important Hungarian director (despite his Italian name). Gregor had been extremely kind to me when I had visited Budapest, so when his friend Basha arrived at my door, preceded by a sugary telephone call, and bearing a tiny Hungarian gift (a little wooden doll) and a typically illegible letter from Gregor, I felt obliged and even happy to welcome her on her "short visit."

I have to admit that I had a slightly ulterior motive in receiving her. For some years, I had been a collector of Hungarian film

24

posters, and I vaguely remembered Gregor mentioning that Basha had some connection (daughter? sister? girlfriend?) to the man who was the guardian of the warehouse in Budapest where all the film posters were stored. It occurred to me that if I were nice to this woman (invited her to a few movie screenings, introduced her to a writer or director or two), she might arrange to have me sent a stack of the latest difficult-to-obtain Hungarian posters.

When she arrived at my house, I was slightly taken aback by her appearance. She had mousey brown hair and glasses and was dressed in a rather drab peasant blouse which she wore loosely over jeans. Not at all the glamorous actress I had anticipated. I invited her in and offered her a glass of wine.

As she looked around my house, I had the uncomfortable feeling that she was making a fast assessment of my wealth and probable importance. It was clear that she had never seen or even heard of any of my films, but, then, I was completely unfamiliar with her work too.

She suggested dinner. I thought we would drive to some little bistro in the vicinity of my house. But she made it clear very quickly that from a Hollywood director, she was expecting something much more grand. Rex? Michael's? Spago? We compromised on an excellent French restaurant in the neighborhood.

As soon as we were ensconced in our booth and the ordering was out of the way (she couldn't decide between two of the most expensive items on the menu and decided to try "a little" of both of them, as well as several appetizers), she started in on a litany of complaints about how hard it was for filmmakers and actresses in particular to function in Hungary: political repression, censorship, sexism and lack of hard currency to buy even color film stock... "Seventy-five dollars? It is not too expensive for a bottle of champagne? Everything taste much nicer...?" she asked, pouting prettily.

I started to answer in the emphatic affirmative, then thought of the generosity and correctness of our friend Gregor and the financial limitations of her country, and ordered the $75 champagne.

While she was making her way through the good-sized lobster, and polishing off the $75 bottle of champagne, she started to tell me about the script she had written herself, "with the help of several friends, *yes, in English,* of course, in English," and which had been tailored precisely to her talents and personality. "Very commercial, of course! Very *romantic, comical, dramatic, intellectual and not expensive* to produce!" She had heard that I sometimes invested in worthy projects. "Perhaps you read my story?" By coincidence, she had a copy with her, which she produced from her voluminous bag with a little alcoholic smile and giggle.

One quick glance was enough to tell me that the script was written in some sort of Hungarian Schoolboy English. There were indications of lots of musical numbers (which, Basha explained, could be made into videos and "make a lot of money").

By this time I was beginning to worry that no possible additions to my poster collection could ever compensate for Basha'a outrageous presumptions, but I was not yet ready to give up completely. Neither was Basha.

"You know, Paul," she said seductively, brushing her leg lightly and provocatively against mine. (I had been waiting for this.) "Gregor has told me *so much* about you! But he made you sound like all work and no playing. Surely you aren't really so serious as all that? Tell me the truth, what do you like to do when you relax and let your hair come down? Do you have many girlfriends?" (Evidently our mutual friend hadn't told her all that much about me.)

It was not, in fact, until she was in the middle of her elaborate, flaming dessert that it became clear to Basha that I was not going to finance her script, she was not going to star in my next film and the thing that seemed to interest me most was not sex, but movies.

"So then tell me, how can I help you with these posters that constantly you are talking about them?" she finally asked crossly.

"Well," I responded, "I seem to remember Gregor telling me that you had a friend or a relative who worked at the poster warehouse in Warsaw."

"Oh, you are speaking of Janos," she sighed. "It is true he used to have posters. As many as you wanted. All this is over. He no longer works at the poster warehouse. He is not in Budapest any more."

"What happened to him? Where is he now?"

"At Hollywood Pacific Motel, waiting for me to bring news you are going to produce my film. He is going to be director."

"You brought him with you to the States to direct you in a film?"

"How should I not bring him? He is my husband. Good directors are easy to find. Good directors who are also good husbands not so easy. Perhaps you will like to meet him? He is very attractive. More your type than me, I think? Maybe you are in mood for a little Hungarian party?! And afterward we can talk about our film project?" Again I felt the pressure of her leg against mine, much less subtly this time.

But by now I was feverishly signaling the waiter to bring the check, counting the seconds before I could say goodbye forever to Basha, and making a mental note that Gregor owed me an expensive dinner and, if possible, a large stack of posters.

Justine Bateman

After seven years playing Michael J. Fox's sister, Mallory Keaton, on *Family Ties,* Justine Bateman returned to the stage to star in *Lulu* at the Berkeley Repertory Theater. Among her other credits are the TV movies *Right To Kill* and *Can You Feel Me Dancing?* and the feature film *Satisfaction.*

When I was a kid, I used to have this dream that my parents weren't my parents. They were these other people who wore masks that looked like my parents. I have the same kind of dreams about whatever guy I'm dating, so my worst date is actually a recurrent nightmare.

I'm at a noisy party and my date suddenly doesn't remember who I am. He doesn't know what the hell I'm doing there or why I'm talking to him. He's nasty. He hates me and he's mean to me. The guy is always some boy I'm in love with, which makes it even more upsetting. I see his face. It's that specific!

He doesn't say anything cruel. He just gives me this look like, excuse me, are you talking to me? Then he turns his back and focuses on another girl, who's probably an old girlfriend of his. Subconsciously I know that's who she is.

Then I find myself running away down a familiar street. I turn a corner and I'm on a street I don't know at all. Both streets look something like 20th Century-Fox's New York street set. I turn around and try to get back to the street that I know, and I never, never, *ever* find the familiar street again.

I'm always on foot. There are no cars around. Nobody can help me. It's day and it's deserted. It feels like one of those *Twilight Zone* episodes where everyone skips years and has the sensation of a complete loss of mind.

And it's all from my point of view. I don't do any reverse shots in my dreams.

The dream ends with me flailing my arms about, screaming, trying to get back through the looking glass, so to speak. But I don't hear any sounds. Not even little dogs. It's quiet and vacant...like a vacuum.

Then I'll wake up and say to my boyfriend, "Are you still here? I just dreamed that you hated me and you didn't know who I was."

He'll say, "It's a nightmare. Don't be worried."

It always happens about six months into the relationship. After that, the relationship gets better. I guess it's my way of making sure that I'm not disappointed by the people I love.

Anne Beatts

CHIP STONE

Anne Beatts was a contributing editor of the *National Lampoon* from 1970 to 1974. She wrote for the original *Saturday Night Live* from 1975 to 1980. Her other credits include: *Square Pegs, A Different World*, and *Julie Brown: The Show*. She has coedited and cowritten several books, including *Titters, Titters 101*, and *The Mom Book*.

I was the original square peg.

I was twelve years old when I started high school and fifteen when I graduated, so I was wearing undershirts when all the other girls were wearing bras, and I certainly didn't know anything about dating. But in characteristic fashion, I tried to confront the situation head on and take advantage of an opportunity to have my first date.

There was a Sadie Hawkins Day square dance at school, so I decided that I would invite Burton—the only human male in my age group who had taken notice of me in a way that seemed more positive than negative—to be my date.

My girlfriend and I had met Burton on a train on one of our "escapes to New York City." We lived in suburban Westchester and we would go into New York City on the train and hang out in the Village because we had this suspicion that this was where real life was going on, even though we couldn't get to it, and certainly no one would have invited us to participate in real life, dressed as we were. Me in my backless wool cocktail dress which my overly indulgent mother had allowed me to buy for school, even though it was totally inappropriate, with bare legs and little flat shoes, and my girlfriend in her little shirtwaist dresses with round collars.

Even though Burton was a high school student like us, he seemed very sophisticated. He told us he was going into the city to take ballet classes. Apparently, he was capable of having a conversation about the finer things in life. The older I get, the more important things like rippling shoulder muscles become, but at twelve I was still interested in pure communication of the mind.

Having rehearsed the phone call with my girlfriend and my mother many hundreds of times, I called Burton up. Much to my surprise he actually seemed to be quite pleased and willing to go.

I then discovered a minor problem. In my enthusiasm, I had invited him to the dance a week early. My mother, who was recently separated (and I guess felt that if she wasn't having a social life, I should have one), suggested that I call him back and say, "Since we were planning to get together anyway, why don't we do something else like go to a movie?"

Gathering the last of my courage, I asked him and, amazingly enough, he agreed. He didn't drive and I certainly didn't drive, so my mother had to chauffeur us to see the only movie that was playing in Bedford Village, *Strangers When We Meet*, with Kirk Douglas and Kim Novak.

After the movie, we had a soda and talked about art while we waited for my mother to pick us up.

I was somewhat disappointed when Burton didn't try and kiss me goodnight. However, having no information about what was supposed to happen on a first date, I was at a loss to influence the situation. If only I had been a married woman having an affair, like Kim Novak in *Strangers When We Meet*, I would have known exactly what to do. But I apparently hadn't done anything really terrible, since he didn't cancel our plans to go to the dance together.

On the following Friday, I put on a very appropriate dress for square dancing. It had a full skirt and a nipped-in-bodice and leg o' mutton sleeves and a square neckline. It was a mustard yellow cotton, covered all over with a tiny flower print. I curled my hair as much as it would curl, trying to achieve the all important flip. My flip was somewhat one-sided—it only flipped on the left—but I thought maybe I could get away with it.

About twenty minutes before the end of the dance, I let go of Burton the ballet dancer's hand and fell flat on my face on the dance floor. It was stunningly embarrassing.

There were only a couple hundred people in the room, but it felt as though the entire world was watching. I wanted to sink into a hole, but I was too numb to move.

It was made all the more humiliating by various people, including the faculty advisors, rushing up and asking, "Are you all right?"

A girl I knew from gym class (she helped me cheat on my gym tests, in return for which I wrote her history compositions) captured my feelings perfectly when she quipped, "Anne, I don't know how someone so smart can act so stupid."

I went home and cried myself to sleep, convinced that I truly was a social dwarf and misfit.

Melvin Belli

Famed trial attorney Melvin Belli has taken on the tobacco industry, General Motors, Coca-Cola, and various governments. He defended Jack Ruby for the murder of Lee Harvey Oswald. Other well-known clients include Mae West, Errol Flynn, Lenny Bruce, The Rolling Stones, Muhammed Ali and Jim and Tammy Bakker.

My parents and her parents arranged it. I had no idea what it was going to be.

They simply told me that I was to dress as Uncle Sam and she was to dress as Miss Liberty. In those costumes, we were to ride on the hood of my family's old Chalmers car in the 1913 Fourth of July parade. Both of us were just about six years old.

We were on show like that, strapped down with a lot of rope and a couple of chairs, waving for two excruciating hours as the parade wound its way from one end of the little town of Sonora, California, to the other. Everybody was on the streets gawking. It was really embarrassing. After the parade we had ice cream and cake at the festivities. Then, because we were a couple, the two of us were left alone.

She was a very cute little girl, I remember. Blond, not too

chubby, a very well-proportioned child. Looks were hardly the problem on this date. I didn't know what I was to do with her.

Since I'd never been out with a girl, I didn't know the protocol. Was I supposed to walk around with her? Talk to her? I guessed I was supposed to let her sit down first. But as an only child, I didn't have anyone to ask for advice.

As a result, we ended up just staying by the grown-ups and talking together somewhat awkwardly. It was the first time I'd ever spoken with a girl in a relatively intimate setting. I didn't know what kinds of things I should be saying to her. The situation was made even more uncomfortable than it already was when older people started coming up to us and saying standard silly things like, "Aren't you cute!" and "What a lovely pair!"

I can't remember what else happened over those two hours, but I do know this first date was my worst date, because it was the one where I had to learn all of the formal rules. After that, I think I've been very lucky with dates—it's my wives that didn't turn out.

Johnny Bench

Elected to the Baseball Hall of Fame in 1989, Johnny Bench won many honors as a top catcher: Ten Golden Gloves, Fourteen All-Star appearances, World Series MVP, National League MVP, and National League Rookie of the Year. He is now a radio announcer and a host of television programs and home videos.

PHOTOFEST

I went out once with a flight attendant whose apartment was possessed by spirits.

She told me she knew them. They came and went, left her messages. I didn't know how much to believe about all of this. She didn't seem to be totally nuts, but, you know, I gave her space.

We went to dinner at a little Mexican place and stopped by some disco for awhile afterwards—nothing real fancy. It was just a comfortable first date except that it was a little spooky, and a lot of fun, just thinkin' about spirits.

When we came back to her apartment and opened the door, she said immediately, "Somebody's been in the apartment." I was somewhat concerned and checked the place thoroughly, as a guy would. It didn't look like anyone had been there to me.

"No, no," she insisted, "that bottle of wine was not there. It was in the other slot." She pointed at this pyramid wine rack sitting on the floor with several open slots. I started to look through the apartment once again, saying, "Maybe you could talk to the spirits. Maybe they'll know who's been here?"

That's actually what she did. She took a pen and she held it by the end between her finger and her thumb, then she put the tip down against a sheet of paper and within seconds, the pen started to write *by itself*. I mean, it actually wrote words! It was slow writing, something like the speed of a Ouija board.

I'm watching her to see if she's doing anything with the pen and I would *swear* that it just wrote by itself. The message the spirit left was something like, "I was here to visit."

I lost my spirit, and my . . . Put it this way, when the writing was done and a couple of minutes had passed, I checked my watch and said, "Gosh I didn't know that it was this late. We've got curfew and I've gotta get back."

I went back to the hotel, but I never went back to her apartment. I figured, why chance it? I'm sure there are other women out there with their own pet spirits who might just like me.

Polly Bergen

Polly Bergen has a successful career in business and show business. Among her business ventures are a cosmetic company, a shoe company and a jewelry company. Her show business experience includes one-woman shows in Las Vegas and Reno, appearances in over thirteen films, and hundreds of television shows, including her own TV series.

I was madly in love with a guy who drove a cab part-time and looked like James Dean. Tall, lanky, devastatingly handsome and very, very sexy.

He knew me, but he didn't notice me, despite the fact that I hung around him all the time and helped him with his homework and did a convincing job of presenting myself as twenty-two, although I was merely seventeen.

When he finally did ask me for a date, I was so excited, I immediately blurted out, "What should I wear?" He said, "Oh, just something very casual."

At seven o'clock, I was dressed and waiting by the door, when I heard the honk of his taxi horn. My father, as usual, grumbled, "Why can't they come to the door and knock like regular people?

Why do they have to honk their horn?" "Dad," I said, "we're running late." You know, the usual lie that kids tell a father who's convinced that every boy who walks through his front door is a rapist, just because *he* was a hellion as a kid.

My date was sitting in his cab looking as beautiful as I'd ever seen him as I opened the front door and started to climb in. He stopped me cold. "You have to sit in the back seat, Polly. I'm working and... well, we've gotta make it look like you're a passenger." Although a bit taken aback by this request, I acquiesced without question and switched to the back seat.

There I discovered a little box. Could this be a gift? Flowers? "I brought a box dinner," he explained. "You know, ham and cheese sandwiches... on white bread." I accepted his explanation with a bewildered, "Oh, that's nice," and settled myself for the ride.

Then he turned on the radio and said, "Look, do you mind if I drop the flag because, like I said, I've gotta make it look like I'm working?"

"Fine."

He dropped the flag and started driving. After a few blocks he pulled out a couple of beers, which was a very racy move at the time. In fact, I'd never had a beer before, but having feigned twenty-two for so long, I wasn't about to admit it.

We drove around like that for one hour and a half—me in the back seat, he in the front, with our sandwiches and our bottled beers.

Finally, he pulled into a dark side street for a few minutes of "talk." I crawled up into the front. He turned off the lights and I knew he was only moments away from trying to get fresh.

I stopped his hand as it inched from my shoulder to my breast with the good girl's battle cry, "What kind of girl do you think I am?" (In those days there were only two kinds.) He looked at his watch. "I really gotta, you know, get going," he said as he started up the motor. "It's been a couple hours... Maybe on one of my nights off we can have another date 'cause I really enjoyed this." "Me too," I swooned.

I continued to glow until we pulled up to my house.

"Polly," he mumbled over the rumbling motor, "the only thing is that uh, uh, you know, I gotta pay this fee and—"

"What are you talking about?"

"Well, you know, I've had uh, the meter going all this time, and I wouldn't want to get caught...and, you know, I can't really cover all of it, so uh, uh, would you split it with me?"

The fee was something like twenty-four dollars, which today would have been the equivalent of one-hundred dollars. Fortunately for him, I had been working with bands since I was fifteen and made a point of never going anywhere without money. We started counting out what I had in my purse, and in the middle of it he said "You know, Polly, I haven't earned any money yet tonight—so I'll tell you what, if you pay for all of it now, I'll cover it sometime during the week?"

I paid the entire fare, which took every dime I had, then I got out of the cab and never saw him again. If this were an isolated incident, it wouldn't have been as memorable. But, *unfortunately*, he was the first of a hundred dates who stiffed me for money.

Anne Bernays

JERRY BAUER

Anne Bernays is an author, teacher, editor and active member of PEN. Her novels include: *Short Pleasures, The New York Ride, Prudence, Indeed, The First to Know, Growing Up Rich, The School Book, The Address Book* and *Professor Romeo.* She is married to Justin Kaplan, the Pulitzer Prize-winning biographer, editor and critic.

We both agree it was a macabre beginning. But perhaps that's what's kept us together for all these years.

I was working for Pocket Books. He was working for Harry Abrams. Pocket Books and Harry Abrams were collaborating on a series of art books so the staff had to interact a bit.

Justin had come over to Pocket Books and chatted briefly with the man I worked with, who, I discovered, was also vaguely related to Justin's family. As he stood there, I noticed his remarkable profile and his emerald green scarf, which he had wrapped around once and let hang down in a studied casual look. I also noticed the shape of his head. It was 1953, the era of crew cuts—It was hard *not* to notice a nice head.

At the time I was always falling in and out of love. My latest amour was the prototype for "John Boy" on *The Waltons*, and we'd been together about six months. As a result, Justin just remained a pleasing image until "John Boy" and I broke up.

I then asked Justin's distant relation if he would arrange a lunch for the three of us.

We went to this restaurant which was entirely white. The floor was white, the tables were white, the tablecloths were white. The windows had long white curtains which were billowing in the light breeze.

It reminded me of the opening scene from *The Great Gatsby*, where everything is described as terribly white and he uses almost nautical imagery. The restaurant evoked that feeling of a sun-bleached, floating room.

The three of us were sitting there having a pleasant conversation when we were privileged enough to experience one of life's memorable comedic episodes. It felt as if it had been lifted out of a slow-motion silent film of one of the great masters: we watched as an Armenian waiter dreased in white brought out a white bowl full of tapioca (Justin claims it was lemon!) soup and instead of placing it on the white tablecloth in front of the man in the white suit who was sitting across from us in the white room, the waiter dropped the soup in his lap. Instantly the man in white rose out of his chair, the waiter hopelessly dabbing with his large white napkin at the huge white stain. The man got more and more angry as the waiter mopped and mopped.

We were all stunned. It was so unexpected, it was almost as if the restaurant had put on a show for us. Justin thought it was hysterical and soon his laughter became infectious. In this state, the conversation then shifted to a murder case which both Justin and I were following with great interest.

A guy who worked in the mailroom at a prominent publishing house and his homosexual lover had been discovered by the mailroom worker's parents. The parents had threatened to prevent their son from receiving some money, so the son and his lover murdered them by making them drink a poisoned daiquiri. Of course they were thrown in jail. As an editor of a literary magazine in addition to my job at Pocket, I had been exposed to a fair number of seedy things, but I wasn't used to murder. Reflecting on these two portions of our first date, one would have thought there wasn't much of a chance for a second one. But somehow we agreed to meet for a second lunch.

This time Justin ordered brains in black butter. I thought to myself, I really like this man and I think I could be very interested in him, but how can I possibly marry a man who eats brains for lunch? First of all, I found the notion of eating brains to be utterly disgusting, and second, brains don't look all that attractive on a plate, they look like brains! It took me twenty years to appreciate them.

Of course I was too polite to say anything to Justin, but I backed up a little bit. He had no idea his choice of cuisine had made such a disagreeable impression on me and was far more concerned about his own shyness and his raging fever, which made him feel like he was about as entertaining to me as a wooden dummy. He didn't mention either problem to me. In fact, weeks later I discovered that he had spent three days in bed with the flu after our lunch.

Looking back, it's hard to believe that two such macabre encounters were the start of what turned out to be a long, steady relationship.

Stephen Bishop

A multiple Grammy award-winning songwriter, Stephen Bishop is also a recording artist, musician, performer, and sometime actor. Formerly with Crosby, Stills and Nash, he has written theme songs for films such as *White Nights*, *Unfaithfully Yours*, and *Tootsie*, for which he won an Academy Award.

Years ago, I was on the road touring by myself with my road manager. We were doing little clubs and I wound up playing this one gig somewhere in Louisiana in this small beach town.

Back then I was just way over the top. I was like a popsicle on acid: I wore a bright, hot pink coat, a turquoise shirt, green pants, and a yellow tie. I was into really being colorful and having a good time.

One of the waitresses at this Louisiana club had great legs. All night I was noticing them. She wasn't Mona Lisa, but she was nice enough.

After the second show, my road manager said, "Okay, Bish, we got to leave here to catch our plane at ten in the morning."

I go, "AAAH. Ten in the morning?"

"Ten in the morning. I'll come pick you up at nine."

I was just about out the door when this waitress with the legs, who I guess had been noticing me noticing her, said, "Hey, sailor, where are you going?"

I said, "Well, it's two-thirty, you know. I've got a plane to catch in the morning."

Right away I knew what was going on. I thought, I've been a lonely guy. This looks pretty promising.

She said, "Well, I've got a little place on the beach. Would you like to see what it looks like?"

I thought, Well, let's see, I can either go up to my room now and get a fairly good night's rest for my gig tomorrow—I *want* to be responsible. I *am* a responsible performer and I *owe* the public a good show—or I can go off with this girl and experience, you know, "seminirvana on the beach," and get one hour's sleep, be miserable, and do the show.

I opted for the second. "Let me get my bag and I'll be right back down."

This is one of my problems in life. I will always go for adventure over what makes sense. Sometimes that has really gotten me into trouble, but usually I've been lucky.

I go up to my room and I get my big Ellesse bag (just in case I need anything with her at the beach), we get into her car and we start driving to her house.

She had given me the impression that her place was five, ten minutes away from the club. I couldn't believe it was so far away! She assured me, "Oh, no. It's coming up. Coming up." Well, she kept saying that, and it was like farther and farther away. I'm thinking, boy is this a big mistake. Big mistake!

About three-thirty in the morning, we finally get to her little place on the beach. But it isn't on the beach. It's actually about a mile from the beach, but you get the beach air. It's part of a row of cottages with a little sidewalk out in front.

I walk into her little, tiny... it is the littlest, the tiniest, the most vulnerable shack, with these huge windows with forty-year-old, flimsy screens that are really loose, and these big, paisley, hippie curtains that are just KURVOOMING with the wind. The whole house is like these curtains going up!

She says, "Can I get you some wine?"

I say, "Sure. What the heck."

In those days, I smoked pot. She had some. I was trying not to smoke to save my voice for the next show, but the ride was sooo long, I smoked a lot. So, I was already bombed when I got to her place and she offered the wine. Really like "zuuuuuu," you know, that "part of the earth feeling"?

I took the wine and we started talking and all of a sudden I hear a noise. All the windows are open, it's really late, and this noise is coming from right outside her door on the sidewalk. It's a *deep, man's voice* and it groans, "Paaatty," which was the girl's name.

Let me tell you, my little hairs on my neck and everywhere just went, "Hello! *Ohhhh godddd!*" It really sounded sinister! And her name was indeed Patty.

She acted like she didn't hear anything. Because I was stoned, it heightened my fear and I got really paranoid. I went, "There is a guy out there and he's saying your name!" He sounds drunk, very drunk, and he growls, "HMMMM GUAGH PAAATTY!"

I go, "Who's that?"

She brushes it off. "He's an asshole. That's who he is."

"Paaatty."

"Do you know this asshole?"

"Patty. Paaaatty."

"Don't worry about him. Just relax. Have some more wine."

I put the wine aside and go, "Wait a minute! What's he doing out there?" (I was trying to regain myself because I was tired after two shows and I didn't want to get anymore untogether than I already was.)

She says, "Forget about him. He's going to go away."

"PAAATTY!"

"Well, he's *still* out there."

I hadn't gotten into a fight since Eddie Helton in sixth grade. I was pretty incredible back then, but it was the sixth grade, you know. I'm a lover, not a fighter—or a songwriter—or something.

I say, "Is he your ex-lover or something?"

"Well...we broke up about a month ago."

"Oh... Did he live here?"

"Yeah, he lived here—for about four or five months with me."

"OHHHHH!"

So I peek out the window to take a look at him and he is this eighties Goliath: with crooked teeth and a balding head and tattoos on his arms. He is big, muscular, and he looks scary. You can't lock the door. The door is this little screen with a paisley curtain. He could just jump right in the window. AHHHH! So I say, "Patty, what's the deal here?"

She says nonchalantly, "Ohhhh, he never got over Vietnam."

I freak. "He never got over Vietnam?!?!? What!!!!"

She dismisses my panic. "He's always pissed off. He's always pissed off!"

"*Paatttyyy!*"

I thought, How am I going to get out of here? It's a small house. I know that she has a back room with a window. Can I get out that window with my big Ellesse bag and run? Run where? I don't know where I am! I am not about to fight this guy over a girl that I barely know.

Meanwhile he's bellowing, "*Patty? Paaatty!* You bitch!"

She goes, "Shut up!" and I start making promises like I used to do when I was young, "Please God, I'll never lie to anyone! I'll be good for the rest of my life!"

She takes charge. "I'm going to talk to him. Everything is going to be fine. Enjoy your wine." Bang. She's out the door.

By this time, I am so nervous I need to find something to defend myself. I reach in my Ellesse bag, and all I can find is my foot massager. A wooden foot massager! Ohhh great, I'll foot-massage him to death.

The arguing out there is getting worse. It sounds like muffled anger. *Angry* muffled anger. Like, "You told me UGHHHHHH. UGHHHHHH! AGGHHRHHH!"

"Why don't you just leave?" she's shouting. "Why don't you just go? What are you embarrassing yourself in front of everybody for!"

He's screaming, "Who is the guy? Who is HE?! Who is THAT MAN? Do I know HIM?"

I go check out the back window in her room. There's nothing but black. I don't know where there's a phone booth, I'm going to miss my gig tomorrow, and I'm going to be in the hospital on top of it.

I come back and sit in the chair right by the screen where they're yelling, and I am thinking, Any minute he is going to throw her down and start raping her or beating her up and I can't let a woman get beat up while I am here. I AM a *man*. I am going to go out there and do something even if I don't really know her or I'm not that crazy about her, right?

So I'm all charged up to do something and they're out there going, "ROARRR ERRRRR!!! HHHHUUUUGGGG ERRRR!," when all of a sudden it's quiet. And she comes back in, "It's all right now. He is going to leave."

"*Ohhh*, is he really?" I am all frazzled to a frick.

Then she picks up the conversation as if nothing had happened, "Yeah, anyway... What were we saying?"

Two seconds later, he hisses from outside, "Hey, sport? Hey, buddy? I wanna talk to ya!" Really angry and vicious and scary. I thought, He must mean *me*. I guess *I'm* "sport."

He taunts, "Come on, sport, come on, sport? Let me say hello to ya. Let me just see ya. Come on, buddy. I'm not going to hurt ya. Let me talk to ya."

With my foot massager in hand, I lean over and put my head in the doorway. Then I go full frame. Him and me. The light is on. I am behind the screen door but he can see me in my hot pink jacket and my turquoise shirt and my yellow tie and everything. I can see him, but not real well. But I see him better than I saw him before, and I am looking into a very large, tall, angry, frothing, Vietnam vet with the tattoos. It is the real thing! I'm thinking, Did I bring enough painkillers in my bag? I wasn't worried about being killed as much as being turned into a pretzel.

As soon as he looks at me, he says, "OHHHH NOOO. Oh, my god...! An ENTERTAINER? Patty, I don't believe it! Well, my opinion of you has gone down, down, down. An ENTERTAINER? Really!"

He looked at me like I was a scum. Mind you, with my bright, pink jacket and my turquoise shirt and my green pants I looked like...An entertainer! I tried to laugh at the insult, but fear still remained my overriding emotion.

For Patty, however, this was the last straw. She stomps back out there, talks to him, and he finally leaves. I can't believe it. I go out there and check, and sure enough, he's gone.

I plead, "Patty, take me back to the hotel. Take me back, please! It's five-thirty in the morning."

She says, "I'm sorry, but I have to wait till Fifi comes back."

"Fifi!?"

I had forgotten about her little, ugly poodle, Fifi. When we first got there, before all this happened, she let the poodle out, saying, "Ohhh, he just roams around the block and he'll be back in a little while." Well, Fifi never came back the whole time she and her ex were fighting.

So I call my road manager hoping he can rescue me, but for some reason, he doesn't answer the phone. I beg her, "Can't we just go?"

"No."

Fifi doesn't show up so finally Patty falls asleep on her bed. I wind up taking off my pants—even though nothing occurred, not even a kiss—trying to fall asleep, too.

Then Fifi comes back and starts FUUURUMFFing the shower curtain. The dog is in love with the shower curtain! I'm in an unknown place. I can't sleep. It's a nightmare!

Finally about 8:30, I feel like death warmed over, I have to catch my plane, I haven't even packed my stuff, I just want to go, I've put on my jacket, I'm starting to put on my pants, when all of a sudden I hear, *"Patty...Paaatty...Paaattttyyy!"* Right at her screen-door window.

AHHHHHHHH It's a daymare!

Last night I survived, now I'm going to die! I was putting on my pants, and now I'm putting them on real quick!

He purrs almost sweetly. "Patty, I love ya. I love ya and I'm sorry. I'm sorry about last night. Paaatty? Patty."

Patty wakes up and barks, "Go away! Just leave me alone!"

He asks, "You got a guy *in there*? Is *that guy* still in there?"

"Yes, HE is!"

"You *BITCH*!!!!"

He goes straight into it. She yells back, goes out there, he leaves again, and we finally drive off.

We didn't talk the whole trip. I didn't want to know this person. AHHHH! How could I have made such an error in judgment? I mean, who is she to be with this guy who eats scrap metal three times a day?

It really taught me a lesson. It taught me to look before I leap. And ever since then, I've tried to talk with my brain before "Little Bish" can get his way.

Nina Blackwood

CHIP STONE

Nina Blackwood was the first MTV video jock. Now the music reporter for *Entertainment Tonight*, she is also cohost of the music/variety program *Solid Gold*.

He was too old for me. He was in his forties, the oldest person I had ever dated, comparatively. But when he asked me to accompany him to his twenty-fifth high school reunion, I cut my vacation in Los Angeles short and flew back to New York City, put on my best dress, and drove with him one hour to Darien, Connecticut.

As soon as we walked in the door of this exclusive club in this exclusive town, we were greeted by an effusive divorcée and her semi-rock-and-roll, eighteen-year-old daughter. She was the only child in the room.

This girl was starstruck. Before I could get her name, she asked, "Do you think you could help me get into the business?"

You know how sometimes you meet people and you just feel like they're taking your essence away? Well, that was immediately how I felt about this girl. Within seconds she sensed my lack of enthusiasm about her future and turned her imploring eyes to my date, who she obviously knew was a successful producer of commercials.

She never left his arm the whole night.

Although she wasn't slated to sit at our dinner table, she, Mom and Mom's boyfriend sat themselves down at our table, placing the enthralled graduating senior on my date's left. I spent the whole dinner having a nice conversation with the mildly confused couple on my right, while inside I'm thinking, Is this my imagination? She's young enough to be his daughter. I must be paranoid. He's too old for mid-life crisis. He's not flirting, he's just being helpful.

He also didn't seem to mind when his classmate asked, "Can you take my daughter home for us?" *Home*? This is a very strange request to make of someone you haven't seen for twenty-five years, regardless of how hot you are for your new boyfriend. However, being the accommodating person that I am, I kept quiet.

We go out to the car and instantly the eighteen-year-old jumps into the front seat, leaving me to climb into the back seat. I wondered if she had bad manners or was just one of those "jump-in" types.

We drive to her mom's condo, park in front, and I feel like I'm sitting in a good seat for a film as I watch my date watch this girl walk up the path to her door. You could just tell from the way he looked at her, he wasn't checking to make sure she was all right. I mean, what's going to happen in twenty feet in Darien, Connecticut?

"Hello, remember me?" I say as I'm climbing over the back seat, "You know, the date you brought with you from New York City? The one you've dated for two years in a mutually exclusive way? Hello?"

The guy berated me from Darien, Connecticut, to New York City. "*You're* crazy, *you're* stupid, *you're* paranoid, *you're* jealous." It was the most horrible one-hour ride I have ever had.

He drops me off at my Manhattan apartment. Doesn't walk me to the door, even though he *knows* several stabbings have previously occurred across the street from *my place*, and I don't hear from him again.

Weeks later I finally get him on the line. "I hired somebody new in the office, somebody you hate." This surprised me. I'm not in the habit of hating people.

Of course it was her. "I couldn't help hiring her," he said. Just like he couldn't help sleeping with her either.

And of course he didn't have the nerve to tell me the truth. One of the other women who worked in his office, who, bless her heart, almost got herself fired for telling me, did. I was devastated. Two years wasted on such a wimp.

A year and a half later, a good friend of mine invited me "as a friend" to his twentieth high school reunion in Kansas City. I went with him just to assure myself that you *can* go to a reunion and *not* be a victim of this kind of disaster.

Dr. Joyce Brothers

Dr. Brothers is a noted psychologist, newspaper and magazine columnist, author, radio personality, business consultant, wife and mother.

This was strictly a deal. We didn't speak on the phone beforehand; he just showed up at my door at seven-thirty on Saturday night. All of this was arranged by his buddy, a terrific guy who had agreed to go out with my infatuated roommate *on condition* that I would date his friend—a guy who had seen me around Cornell but didn't have the nerve to ask me out on his own.

I can see why he might have been intimidated. I was supremely popular in college. There was always a crowd of men around me and I was dating lots of the best "big men on campus."

When I opened the door that night, I was frozen in place. My blind date was about my height, five-one, roly-poly in build, and had six tiny, Marcel fingerwaves across the top of his forehead. They looked just like the type of waves women worked hard to create with hairnets and bobby pins.

He was the original nerd, except we didn't have a word for nerd in those days.

He had very tall socks that compensated (probably accidentally) for his very short pants. His jacket looked like the blankets the ponies wear in Central Park. Although I was already studying psychology, my training didn't quell my intense and immediate desire to escape to the movies. Unfortunately, he had already seen the only movie playing in the college town of Ithaca, New York, and though I racked my brain for an alternative dark spot, the only thing that came to mind was a place to neck. Since that was certainly not what I was interested in doing, there was no choice but to go someplace where we would be seen.

We wound up at J.P.'s, the local college hangout, where it seemed like all 10,000 people at Cornell were eating that night. Included among them were *all* the men I'd been dating all over campus.

I didn't live this date down for forty years.

Now this man's looks wouldn't matter to me at all, but when you're a sophomore in college, they are of paramount importance.

The saddest thing about the date was its consequences for my roommate. The supposedly terrific guy had actually relieved himself of all future responsibility to my girlfriend, because he knew with certainty that I would never go out on a second date with his buddy.

David Brown

David Brown, in partnership with Richard D. Zanuck, produced films such as *Jaws*, *The Sting*, *The Verdict*, *Cocoon* and *Sugarland Express*. For years, Brown and Zanuck headed film production at 20th Century-Fox, and later at Warner Brothers. He continues to produce plays, films and TV series.

I was a lonely young man in New York at a time when men outnumbered women. It was before the war. And I was taken by a romantic phrase that I read in the personal ad section of *Saturday Review of Literature*. "Girl with windswept hair who loves Mozart, horseback riding, long walks in the country, and wine, seeks man with equal sensitivity and romantic interests. Svelte, sensuous, exceedingly young, nineteen-inch waist, great legs." A knockout.

In the late thirties, we were all on the lookout for sexual adventures. The sexual revolution hadn't taken place and this ad looked like the realization of a great fantasy. Especially to a humble *Women's Wear Daily* reporter, just out of college, with no money and one suit. I was living at the Winslow Hotel at 55th Street and Madison Avenue, paying, I think eight or nine dollars a week for a single room so small that if you opened the door, you fell over the bed. It wasn't the kind of place where one could bring even a woman who wrote this type of ad. As soon as she saw the place, my intentions would be obvious.

Undaunted, I answered the ad.

At the appointed hour, I waited for my date outside the French restaurant I had chosen on West 55th Street. The moment I saw her coming, I panicked. She was twice my size, three times my width and much older than I was. "Wait, I just remembered something," I said to her. "This restaurant has been cited for giving its customers ptomaine poisoning. Let's go somewhere else."

I could ill afford it, but we got into a taxicab and I took her to a restaurant in the farthest reaches of Brooklyn, somewhere no one I knew would see me. I thought, What am I doing with this giant? She could have been all of thirty, but to me, at twenty-one, she was "mother."

The cab ride almost wiped me out; there were no credit cards in those days. By ordering only tea on the pretext of not being hungry, I managed to pay the check. She was a nice woman, but her description of herself would have caused her to be indicted for deceptive advertising!

I never brought up the discrepancy. It would have been ungallant. I simply made small talk with a very large woman.

Today I cringe at the thought of my behavior. If I were to do it all again, I would never be so rude as to hustle her out of a restaurant. Secondly, I would request a photo.

After lunch, I took her home, said it was wonderful.

She telephoned me once. I said, "Look, I'm being transferred to Cleveland." That was the end of it. I didn't break her heart and she certainly didn't break mine.

As a result of this experience, I never answered another personal ad. I still read them, however.

Helen Gurley Brown

Editor-in-chief of *Cosmopolitan* for twenty-five years, Helen Gurley Brown is the best-selling author of six books—*Sex and the Single Girl, Sex and the Office, The Outrageous Opinions of Helen Gurley Brown, Helen Gurley Brown's Single Girl's Cookbook, Sex and the New Single Girl* and *Having It All*. She is married to producer David Brown.

I'm a profound believer in blind dates. I think it's something that you owe your friends, especially if you're married and you know a lot of people and you get around. That's how I met my husband and how I met many of the men I dated during the eighteen years I was single. It's also how I met my worst date.

I can't remember if I was in the stage where your friends think you're so desperate—you won't care if the man is Sam Shepard or Robert Dole or whoever your ideal man is at the time—I just remember my girlfriend telling me he was a hunk. A young Charlton Heston type, if you remember what he looked like in *Ben Hur*.

She also told me he came from a good New England family. Because I was then living in Los Angeles and working at one of my seventeen secretarial jobs, this all sounded very substantial to me. He wasn't a looney tune from Hollywood, or the outskirts of Long Beach or Ventura, he was Boston aristocracy! With this man I'd have no qualms running into my boss.

The Bostonian selected a lovely restaurant on Sunset Strip, which was known as a very glamorous and very appropriate place to take a girl. This all sounded quite promising.

We sat down and ordered drinks. After a minimum of polite conversation, the big hunk keeled over and went to sleep on the tablecloth, somehow avoiding his double vodka martini on the descent. If he hadn't started to snore, I would have thought he'd had a heart attack.

I assume he was probably soused before he picked me up, although I certainly didn't perceive it. I was always naïve about such things. He didn't slur his words and the conversation hadn't gotten involved enough for me to notice that two and two was adding up to seventeen instead of four.

When he didn't come around on his own, I tugged at his sleeve. It did absolutely no good.

Then I spoke at him across the table. This only served to arouse the further interest of the adjacent diners, who were whispering to themselves, "Poor, poor girl, what is she doing out with this sleeping giant on her hands?"

Next, I hit him across the back of the shoulders. This merely elicited a couple of grunts that caught the attention of the captain, who rushed to my rescue. I don't know whether he used a cattle prod to awaken him, but he suddenly snapped his head back and acted for an instant like everything was normal. Of course, he had the waiter there to help him along: "I think you two would probably like the gazpacho and the veal..."

Later, when he tried to order a bottle of wine, the management refused to serve him. Even then, he didn't get obstreperous; he was a properly educated New England man.

I drove both of us to my home in his car.

When I got out, I said goodnight, told him how to get back on the freeway and hoped for the best. I just thought I'd been through enough disappointment that night, I didn't have to try and protect the rest of society from this oaf.

It was a wasted evening. Still, I tend to be a rather forgiving person when it comes to men. After all, they're our only other sex. What are you going to do? They're not perfect.

Rae Dawn Chong

Rae Dawn Chong has appeared in a diverse group of films including *Loon, The Principal, Soul Man, Commando, The Color Purple, Beat Street, Choose Me* and *Quest for Fire*.

Let's see, I think a bad date is anybody who arrives stoned or drunk or anyone who gets stoned or drunk while I'm on the date. And another bad date is anyone who insists that I go dutch or pay. And another bad date is anybody who tries to kiss me, oh, before dinner. And another bad date is anybody who tries to impress me with what he knows about wines; I think that's really disgusting. And another bad date is anybody who takes you to one of those torturous, four-star restaurants where there're seventeen courses and insists you try everything. I mean that's like hell. And another bad date is anybody who wants to take you shopping for clothes for them, yuck. And another bad date was one I had while I was doing preparation work for *Quest for Fire.*

I met this beautiful guy in Paris who was fresh off a kibbutz. He was just gorgeous: blond, curly hair, very Israeli, you know, that Jewish-American, poetic stunner. Dark overcoat, jeans, sweatshirt. Just nice, very artistic.

We had espressos and everything was glamorous and fabulous and sensuous, but unfortunately he was leaving the next day.

So we made a date for Los Angeles where we both lived. I was sad because you know how Paris can be: they're either selling you burnt bagettes, or they're telling you how much they love you, or they're telling you how revolting you are.

When he came to pick me up in Los Angeles he was, first of all, driving a souped-up Camaro. He had on platform shoes with three or four inch high heels, (This was in the late, late seventies, early eighties, so they were way out of style.) He had on a belt that wrapped around his waist, then around his left thigh, and he insisted that we go to Burger King.

I was all dressed up and so disappointed. I just stood there, stunned, looking at this apparition, and decided that this was not for me.

I ended a lot of dates at the door at the time, surprisingly enough. I don't think he was shocked. Actually, I think he felt that the second I laid eyes on him whatever chemistry that was there in Paris was left in Paris.

I did see him once after that, at a wedding, six or seven years later. He wasn't wearing his thigh belt, but he did have something adorning his body that was equally revolting.

Didi Conn

HARRY LANGDON

Actress Didi Conn's films include *You Light Up My Life*, *Grease I*, *Grease II*, and *Violet*. She appeared regularly on such TV shows as *Benson* and *Shining Times Station* with Ringo Starr.

It was 1966, I was fifteen years old, and my hormones were really kicking in. I mean, I was reading *Candy* in the bed and getting all excited, but I didn't attract boys like my idol, Donna.

Donna had this kinda flair, this aura. Even if she was wearing jeans, she always looked sexy. We were the same age, but she had skipped a grade, so she had already been in high school and was dating lots of older boys. I kept saying, "Please, Donna, I want to do what you do." Finally, Donna offered to fix me up with one of her guys, Junior Salico. The name sounded scary, but it also sounded sexy.

Right away I got worried, 'cause I knew the first thing my Jewish parents would ask was, "What's the boy's last name?" "Junior Schwartz?" People don't call themselves "Junior" when they're Jewish, right?

Plus he had a car. I made up this whole story: that I already knew this guy, that he was a driver's ed teacher, but that he was only seventeen year's old, 'cause I couldn't go out with anybody too old, either. I guess my parents were depressed and desperate for me to go out, because they bought this story.

That night, I put on what was like a dress-up outfit for me: my blue cheerleader jacket, my plaid skirt, a peter pan collar blouse with a little round pin at the neck and my good yellow sweater. I looked like this very collegiate Catholic schoolgirl, although I thought I looked sexy.

So I'm waiting in the kitchen for this guy, and I realize I'm scared to death. You know, here I was, lying so much that I didn't understand the weight of the situation: that I was going on this blind date with Junior Salico. What if the wrong person came to the door? Like this killer. You know, Junior Salico would bail out and send his Uncle Mario or something. I said to myself, "Didi, you got to do something here." So, I took a knife.

It was just this little steak knife with a green plastic handle. To me, this could kill someone. Probably couldn't even cut London broil. In fact, my father used to always yell about that. He hated those knives.

But, anyway, I put it in my pocket. And sure enough, this swarthy, looking, sexy, Italian guy comes hunking up to my door. He's like older and he was wearing, you know, Italian clothes: leather jacket, white shirt, the smear. I don't remember seeing hairs on his chest—I remember looking for them. He goes, "What would you like to do?" I say, "Why don't we go to Marine Park?"

Now Marine Park is where my friends would go when we were in junior high. There's lots of swings and monkey bars. You play around. And you swing. And you have a good time.

So he goes, "Really? You want to go to Marine Park?" I say, gaily, "Yeah, great."

Little do I know that that's where people go to park, not to play.

Junior's getting all excited. I'm all happy, cracking jokes, and thinking, Oh boy, this is a fun guy. Why was I so worried?

We get to Marine Park and he parks the car, and I still don't notice that there's, like, a lot of cars around with smoked-up windows. He goes, "Well, here we are." I go, "Yeah, I'm so glad you took me here," and I start to get out the door.

He says, "Where are you going?" I say lightly, "Haven't you been here before? I'll take you to the swings."

"Yeah... I've *been here* before. What do you mean, take me to the swings?" Then he starts laughing like I'm a comedian and moves a little closer.

I say, "Wait a minute. Really. I'm serious. There's these great monkey bars!"

"Ha ha ha. Monkey bars." And he keeps getting closer.

I realize something's up here. He ain't getting out of the car. I start to really get panicked and I say, "Listen, Junior, I got a knife."

He says, "What?"

I say once again, "I got a kniiife," in this silly little voice, trying to be threatening.

He doesn't believe me. "If you have a knife," he says, "I'll take you home right now." So I take out the knife and he goes from Rocky Balboa to this ghost.

As he's recovering, he asks, "Why did you do that?"

I whine, "'Cause I didn't know who you were, and I got all upset..."

"Oh, baby... Don't be upset," he says sweetly.

Then salami de l'amore over there starts kissing me anyway! Stainless steel doesn't stop this guy.

I'm like, "Oh, no, oh, no. I don't want to be here. I don't want to do this." I'm a cold fish, but I'm panicked. So I say, "Can't you put the radio on?" He barks back, "I don't have a radio!" It was obvious he didn't have a radio and he thought I was needling him, trying to hurt his macho pride. I try to cover up my mistake, "Well, since you don't have a radio, I'll sing. 'Imagine me and you, I do. How I think about you day and night. Happy Together.'"

I mean, I'm still trying levity here, it's only making things worse. This guy was pissed! This wasn't what he expected *at all*.

He just took me home. No food. No nothing. He didn't like my singing voice, I guess. At least that's what I told my idol, Donna.

I never went armed with a knife to a date again. Although I certainly went armed with more excuses.

Alice Cooper

COURTESY OF CBS RECORDS
GLEN LA FERMAN

The Dracula of Rock and Roll once said about himself: "When everyone else was into peace and love, Alice Cooper was into fun, sex, death and money."

For some reason, the staunch-hearted Alice Cooper was scared to see *The Exorcist*. I don't know why. I was a horror movie junkie when I was a kid, absolutely, and I still am. My show is a total horror film. I mean, when you think of Alice Cooper, doesn't it look like dripping letters? I tried to make the name synonymous with Baby Jane and Lizzie Borden. It worked, but it still didn't give me the courage to see *The Exorcist*. It was like I don't know, something about it.

Then I met Linda Blair at somebody's party and told her I would only see the movie if she would go with me. She said, "Okay, let's go tomorrow night."

I don't know what I thought was going to happen. To be honest, I just thought it would be a funny idea—Alice Cooper taking Linda Blair to *The Exorcist*. It was like Dracula of Rock and Roll takes out the Possessed.

I sent a limo to pick her up. From Linda's reaction, I don't think she had had a lot of star treatment before this. To me, it seemed like a normal thing. I was always taking limos places. I didn't drive at all. (At least I was smart enough not to drive.) This was back in "the blackout days" when I used to drink, like, a bottle a day, but I was always a gentleman. A happy drunk. (Now I don't drink at all.)

Then the limo picked me up. I got in and discovered Lenny Bruce's daughter was there, too. Kitty Bruce. So the three of us went to a theater here in Hollywood somewhere.

I was always Alice when I went out at that time. Now, it just depends on where I'm going. If it's a professional thing, like I'm going to a concert, I'll go as Alice, not with the full makeup, but you know, with the Alice persona. If I go to a baseball game, I tie my hair back and try to disguise myself so I don't have to sit there and sign autographs for eight hours. Back then, I always wore black leather and at least enough black mascara to make my eyes dark. My hair was long, black, and elegantly ragged, very Cooperesque. I was definitely Alice Cooper that night.

So picture this: Alice Cooper and Linda Blair standing in line to pay to get in, right? It was sort of like the Addams Family goes to the movies. You know, we feel perfectly normal, like the Munsters think they're totally normal, because we live with ourselves every day.

But to everyone else this was scary. Remember, this was the time when people were throwing up and passing out during my show (that was, at least, the press), because we had a lot of blood and a decapitation on the stage. We were the first to do it. And we were the first to really do it on the level of extravaganza.

Until that night, I didn't realize that Linda was fifteen! I only realized it when she and Kitty started giggling. All, *all*, ALL they talked about was *Rick Springfield*! They were just in love with him or infatuated with him. It was giggling about Rick Springfield the whole time! I might as well not have been there, except that I was, you know, their escort. I was only about twenty-five myself at the time, but I felt like I was their fifty-six-year-old dad.

To cope, I started to guzzle the bottle of VO I'd smuggled into the theater. They kept tittering about Rick Springfield and I kept trying to ask Linda technical questions like, "How did you make your head spin around? What about that crucifix?" People kept going SHHHH! Then they would turn around and they would see who they were talking to... I mean, in that movie, at that time, if somebody was on LSD or something, they were probably terrified.

But the best part of all was watching the crowd leaving the theater. They had just gotten their breath back and then they'd see Linda Blair. They were shocked, but trying to be cool. Then they'd see me and it was a double package. It was so funny. Because this was also at the point when parents would hide their children when they saw Alice Cooper in airports.

After the movie, nothing happened. We didn't have much in common other than trouble with our heads. But that's okay. I forgive her teenaged crush. Then again, maybe she thinks I was her worst date.

David Copperfield

Four-time Emmy Award-winner David Copperfield combines old-style magic with high-tech wizardry in his dazzling illusion shows. He has toured the U.S. and the world numerous times, appeared on Broadway, and produced twelve specials for CBS.

I always like dates to Disneyland and Disney World because they allow me to see the different colors a woman has: Can she have fun on the worst rides as well as the best rides? Can she still act like a child? Sometimes I like to be like that, and I think it's nice if a woman can be that way too. There's also something very romantic about the Magic Kingdom.

About a year ago, a model with intriguing eyes and a great sense of humor and I decided to have our first date at Disney World. Since she lived in New York and I'm always on tour, we flew in separately and planned to meet by the entrance at ten AM.

I waited patiently for her at the park entrance until noon, but she didn't show. I had her paged. No response. Anxious, I called her hotel room. There was no answer. I decided to search for her on foot. I walked through the entire park looking for her, but she was nowhere to be found. Now, thinking she had either stood me up or missed her flight, I decided to at least go on some of my favorite rides since childhood, such as Pirates of the Caribbean and the Haunted Mansion , so that the day wouldn't be a total disaster.

Meanwhile, everyone around me was a having a great time. Young couples seemed to be everywhere holding hands, talking and laughing, completely ignoring me. (Disney World isn't the kind of place where single ladies tend to hang out.) So, I spent the entire day dragging myself all around the happy Magic Kingdom, alone.

Finally, five minutes before closing time, my date showed up. She was so elated to find me standing at the gate, she ran up and kissed me, then apologized profusely. She had missed her flight, was trying to get another one, and just couldn't. Relieved that she was okay, I grabbed her, and we ran around like maniacs, laughing and having fun, as we tried to squeeze in as many rides as we could. Peter Pan, Haunted Mansion, Space Mountain, Pirates of the Caribbean, and more, all in a frenzied five minutes. She was a determined trouper, who was certainly worth the all-day wait!

As we were leaving, I overheard the guy in the Mickey Mouse costume saying, "That's David Copperfield, the magician. He ought to slow down and enjoy himself! You can't just bring a girl to the park and expect to see everything in five minutes!"

I certainly didn't see everything about her in five minutes. We went on several dates, and the next time, wouldn't you know, *I* was late.

Ted Danson

Star of NBC's *Cheers*, Ted Danson is a versatile actor whose most recent films include *Dad*, *Cousins* and *Three Men and a Baby*. He won a Golden Globe for his dramatic role in *Something About Amelia*.

I went to Kent Prep School for Boys, so my dating years were severely curtailed. In fact, it was only about once every two months, when Kent had a dance with one of the girls' schools in Connecticut, that anything had the possibility of happening.

Nothing much did. Kent was very backward during the time I was there. If you held hands, that was kind of risqué. And if you got too close while you were dancing, there were people with rulers who would separate you. So, it was not good for dating at all.

The girls for these dances were bussed in about eleven in the morning on Saturday. Saturday afternoon, you'd watch the football game together. After that you'd have dinner, and in the evening, there would be a sock hop in the gym. By nine o'clock they were back on the busses to go home.

This in itself wasn't the bad part of the arrangement. The *bad part* was how they chose your date for you.

You would get assigned a date by height. It was just like the army. They'd call off your name as the girls got off the bus. Ted so and so. Carole so and so.

My first couple years I was very foolish and told the truth about my height. I was six-two at fifteen, which meant I inevitably ended up with the girl who was six foot.

The one saving grace of the day, however, was something very cruel called "the Moose Pool." Each of the sixty boys at Kent would put in fifty cents. If you had the ugliest date, by mutual consent, you would receive "the Moose Pool." This was '64, '65, so $30 was a sizable amount of money.

One weekend, I put in my money, and, sure enough, my date emerged from the school bus and she was six foot. A big six foot! She was a lacrosse player. We had nothing in common. Nothing.

As scheduled, I took her to the football game and was in a pretty grumpy mood. We went to dinner, and as I looked around at my buddies and their dates, I started to lighten up because I realized I'd just probably won "the Moose Pool."

Then, when the girls were about to get on the bus to go home, I felt kind of bad because I knew I should have been nicer to my date. I mumbled something like, "I'm sorry it didn't turn out that well."

She smiled and chirped, "Oh, that's okay, because I won the Moose Pool."

I couldn't believe it! The girls had a "Moose Pool" going, too, and she had won!

It was a wonderful comeuppance. And I think it threw me off girls for the next three years. During which time, I played basketball with my buddies and watched *short* people go on *great* dates.

Jon S. Denny

FRAN KUHN

Jon S. Denny is the creator and producer of the widely acclaimed PBS series *Trying Times*. Mr. Denny also produced the feature films, *Nobody's Fool* and *The Object of Beauty*. Eventually he would like to join the Supreme Court.

We are the smartest and most advanced of all living things, and are the only creatures on earth who know that someday each of us will die. That sort of puts a crimp in any evening, as far as I'm concerned. Still, I've always tried to enter into dating conditions with a reasonable distillation of hope, good cheer and cologne. However, I am still filled with dread when I recall a couple of instances of social intercourse, which left me wondering if I would be better off in an immersion tank.

The first date from hell (a blind one, actually) took root in Los Angeles, which is depressing enough in itself. Said blind date showed up in a dress which looked like a painting Picasso threw out, and then proceeded to punch me in the arm every time she said something she thought was amusing. From the welts on my arm the next day, you would've thought that I dated Jackie Mason. At the end of the night, it was apparent that this rather coquettish, curly-haired female was in fact severely sad, and that her jabs of ingratiation were a part of her denial system. I spent at least three hours trying to convince her not to commit suicide, and then we reached an impasse by agreeing that her main problem was that her spine was out of alignment. At quarter of four in the morning, she called the man who rolfed her, who turned out to be her fiancé, and who showed up at her place on a moped. I decided it was time to leave.

But I suppose the most terrifying rendezvous of all was with a particularly alluring free-lance writer and part-time Zoli model, who contributed think pieces on eye creams to such disparate publications as *The Christian Science Monitor* and *Seventeen.* She wore lacy gloves, white high heels, and a corset which interrupted her breathing pattern. The first sign of danger was when I noticed a lime streak in her hair.

I took her to a great and venerable old Italian restaurant on the west side of New York, where all the waiters predate Mussolini and claim to know Vic Damone. We ordered clams casino, white wine and red mostaciolli, a dish resembling veal, a vat of meat sauce, and a couple of dinner salads with megacholesterol dressing. Most models I know eat bark and water for dinner, so I was glad to be with a woman who may have actually once eaten a Pop-Tart. Unfortunately, food is where the real trouble began.

My date picked at her salad with a strange look in her contact lens, and then spent the next hour trying to set fire to an olive. She tried with a match, she tried with a Bic. God knows, she even tried with a candle. I don't know which law of physics or foodstuffs she was trying to apply, but it is in fact impossible to set fire to an olive. It is, however, entirely possible to set fire to a tablecloth. She said it was an accident. Mario the waiter put out the blaze with San Pellegrino.

Undaunted—and on the way back to my apartment on the fashionable East Side—we passed a firetruck hurtling in the opposite direction. She thought it would be fun to give chase. Ninety-seven blocks later, I realized the meter was running. The cab ride cost me more than dinner.

The end of a glorious, star-filled night was spent watching three overweight firemen who didn't tuck in their pants attempting to extinguish a minor blaze in a Korean fruit stand. I think one of the pomegranates caught on fire. Or one of the olives.

As a general rule, I don't think it's a wise idea to get involved with a woman whose idea of a nice time is third-degree burns.

Alan M. Dershowitz

Dubbed by *Time* magazine "the top lawyer of last resort in the country," Harvard Law School Professor Alan Dershowitz is a prolific author of articles and books, including *The Best Defense* and *Reversal of Fortune: Inside the Von Bulow Case*. He frequently contributes his legal opinions to radio, television and print interviews.

I was a pretty bad kid at the yeshiva, the Jewish parochial school in my neighborhood. The kind of troublemaker that is commonly known as a "bundit," a brat. All the parents knew about what kind of terrible kid I was. So, I figured, when I wanted to go to the prom, I might encounter a little resistance. Luckily, I had my eye on Karen, this sexy blonde from the next neighborhood. I hoped her parents wouldn't know about my rotten reputation.

At the yeshiva, we were not allowed to pick our own dates. There was a *committee* established to *arrange* the dates!

I went up to the committee, I'll never forget... There they were, sitting like three queens: Barbara, Helene and Gladys. I stood there and I looked at them. And I said very, very nervously, "I'd like to go to the prom with Karen."

All three of them burst out in hysterical laughter. "Don't you realize," they snapped haughtily, "Karen is on the A list. *You* are on the C list. You can't go with her!"

It turns out, they'd ranked everybody in the school... on the A, B, C, and also, I fortunately learned, D list. At least I wasn't on the D list.

But according to persnickety Barbara, I was on the C list and could only pick a prom date from either one list above, B, or one list below, D. A list-Karen was not an eligible date for me.

I looked through the lists of people and found that the only acceptable person on the C list or B list was one of my cousins. So I ended up going to the prom with my cousin, who was a very nice "date."

The prom itself was terrible. At some point, I went over to Karen and asked her to dance. She snubbed me. She knew I was permanently on the C list (as did everyone else in the school.)

That was my first and last attempt at social climbing.

Pamela Des Barres

Pamela Des Barres became notorious with the publication of her bestselling rock 'n' roll memoir, *I'm With the Band.* She now writes a column for *Request* magazine and is a frequent contributor to *Cosmopolitan* and *Details.*

Pamela and then husband Michael Des Barres

My mom was mortified when she opened the door. She knew I'd met him in New York on the set of *Arizona Slim*—this movie I was starring in that never came out—when he replaced Keith Moon—who didn't show up—and we had to scour New York for an English rock 'n' roll person who could act. We found him touring with the glitter band called "Silverhead."

She also knew that he had called me at a sort of boyfriend's house several days earlier and told me he was going to jump off the Hyatt House roof if I didn't let him see me right then. I told him he was gonna have to jump because I wasn't leaving the cowboy, my sort of boyfriend, that night to see him.

So when Michael Des Barres showed up at my mom's house the next day, bombed out of his mind, wearing a silver lamé jumpsuit, zipped down as low as it would go, with two bottles of Southern Comfort, one in each pocket, and his chipped fingernails painted every color of the rainbow, she wasn't too anxious to take him up to see me in my "ex-bedroom," where I was curled up under the covers in my red cotton nightie with the flu. He knew I'd be there because I'd told him I always tried to recuperate with Mom when I had a little too much of life.

I was thrilled to see him.

Mom left us alone. We closed the door and started listening to some music. Some time later Mom kind of tapped on the door, opened it, and caught Michael with his head under my nightie, having a little fun. She went, "Oh, excuse me," and shut the door.

I was a little embarrassed. Michael wasn't. But I figured Mom already knew what a wild lunatic I was, and that I had to have pretty much what my heart desired at any moment. Still, I felt bad for her, she's such a doll. I mean, she'd never even seen this guy before. On the other hand, what could she say? It was 1974 and I was a twenty-five-year-old woman.

I guess she must have waited for me in the hallway or something, because as soon as I walked out of my bedroom, she said, "Pamela, come, I wanna see you in the kitchen."

We went into the kitchen and she sat me down and she said, "You're not serious about this one, are you?" I hadn't told her that Michael had already asked me to marry him the day I met him and I was seriously thinking about it, so I said, "I, I, I... think so."

She just looked at me and I thought, This is a great date for me, but this is a real bad date for my mom.

A couple days later I moved to the hotel with Michael and we got married not too long after that.

Gavin Geoffrey Dillard

STEVEN ARNOLD

Having left Asheville, North Carolina, and the South behind, Dillard is an Angelino enroute to Hawaii. Author of six books of poetry, he has also written songs for and with Peter Allen, Bruce Roberts, Donna Summer and Sam Harris.

Back at the turn of the century—about 1980—you remember, when white people still did drugs, I was flown to Aspen in a private jet to attend a New Year's Eve weekend ski party thrown by Barry Diller, Sandy Gallin, Calvin Klein and I can't recall who else. It was an all-star weekend, to be sure, with Cher, John Denver, Jack Nicholson, Neil Diamond, Dolly Parton and most anybody you wanted to see in 1980. A group of us settled into a large modern home belonging to Ed Wynn.

I won't say what anybody else's condition was, but I was rather inebriated by the time we left the houses to go skiing. As I recall, plans were rather spontaneous, but somebody said, "Well, you two can't ski, so you guys go off together and do the beginner's slope." They all wanted to do the grown-up slopes. So after five minutes of instructions on how to stop, there I was alone on the baby slope with Barbra Streisand.

Well, I was delighted, and certainly too stoned to be intimidated by Ms. S.—whom I had had perhaps more than one fantasy about in this lifetime—but to all of a sudden be alone with the woman, without any warning, WAS an experience. There she was, no makeup, a sock over her head, a rather dated-looking fuschsia knit jumpsuit, totally subdued, and she STILL turned heads on the slope. I mean, you see the profile stumbling past you and you just KNOW. So, wobbly as I was, I was dutiful and stuck close between her and anyone else. I've been out with Bianca Jagger, Lily Tomlin, Jane Fonda and other divas as well as my buddies Bud Cort and Paul "Pee-wee Herman" Rubens—so I'm aware of a certain decorum, especially necessary with the ladies—but this was like escorting MS. GOD.

To boot, she was a horrible skier, which made an already improbable low profile impossible. I did pretty good, I think because I was too stoned to care—but poor Babs was panicked. Ninety percent of the time, as I remember it, was spent pulling her by the ankles out of endless snowdrifts. Not exactly what many would call romantic. She could've had a sense of humor about it, but I think she felt abandoned and blackballed by the whole set-up. And I know she caught me laughing once or twice.

I tried to be friendly, perhaps too friendly, but it all just fell flat, you know. Every line just dropped into the snow and sat there as we edged downward. By the end of our allotted time together she didn't even acknowledge my existence, other than as a sort of walking ski pole and emergency brake.

That night, at the New Year's bash in a local restaurant, I somehow jostled from Barbra's table over to that of Neil and Marsha Diamond. Okay, so we got off to a bad start, big deal.

By the end of the evening I was in no position to feel ANY remorse. Two days of drinking, smoking, ingesting assorted white powders had put me into my own little movie of cameos and easy-listening conversations. A group of us staggered back to the house and I was looking forward to ten hours of darkness when I was ushered into a room and rather tossed into a bed that was full of Dolly Parton.

THERE SHE WAS—both of her—in a baby blue negligee. Another fantasy come true, my favorite country singer, one of the sexiest women I've ever known. And I'm thinking, Ohhh, I'm really tired now. Ohhh, I really feel like shit. Ohhh, it's been a really scary day.

Dolly, however, is one of the sweetest, most spontaneous and down-home people you'd ever want to meet. "Pull up a pillow and sit down!" she said as she whipped her guitar out from under the double bed, and without asking proceeded to play four or five new songs that she had been working on.

One of them was called, "My name is Andy" and was about a little orphan and a dog and a snowstorm. "It was," as she put it, "plum pitiful." But charming. I'm a sucker for that kind of music.

She was delightful. Totally upfront—so to speak. A perfect hostess. We talked about our childhoods, just across the mountains, the weather in the South, and most any trivia available to us at the time and state of night.

But I must say, I was a zombie. It was painful keeping the lids up. Even thinking where I might like to let my fingers ramble across her strings. Dolly in her next-to-nothing nightie that was a tad old-fashioned, frilly and innocent. Not a vamp at all, she was new in Hollywood and still very Nashville. Casual as could be except for full makeup and the wig that she informed me doesn't come off until the door is locked and the lights are out. That made sense—it would be like seeing Barbra without the nose. Anyway, I liked the wig. That's half the woman.

Well, the inevitable happened. Somewhere between the songs and the conversation, little Gavin was out for the count—gone, dead. It was well into the next day before I had any cognition of existence at all. And by then the angel Dolly was off enjoying her vacation without me.

I never asked her how she slept—or where. No one else bothered to press either of us for details. Dolly was, as ever, charming and witty about the house and town. I suppose I could have joked about "how I was," but this day, frankly, I was embarrassed, and frustrated that I had flunked out of star f—ing 101, that I had missed half the vacation. It was, after all, the end of the seventies—that whole decade we all sped and barbed our way through. Discos, real estate and one-night stands.

Nevertheless, I would have at least liked to have seen Dolly without her wig...

Jonathan Elias

©JACOB GETZ

Jonathan Elias is a record producer and composer who began by writing music for commercials that won ten Clios and twenty gold awards at Cannes. His eleven feature film scores include *Parents* and *Shakedown*; his work for TV includes *The Brain* for PBS. As a record producer he has worked with Duran Duran and Grace Jones.

I spotted the tattoo on her back from across the room. She was tall, gorgeous and sealed in a rubber dress. I soon found out her name was Arielle—she said she was a European model.

There were always a lot of models at those horrible music industry parties, as well as a bunch of flacks and A&R people. I was there with the British pop star I was working with at the time. The party didn't make me feel anything like the name of the bar, "Hot Diggity Dog."

With some heavy arm-twisting by the pop star, I got up the nerve to ask Arielle out. She tossed her long locks over her shoulder and purred that she would love to. She then surprised me by saying that she would pick me up the next night about nine o'clock.

The next evening, I was so excited that I was dressed and ready by seven-thirty. She showed up a little after midnight, but she was in a stretch. Neither the hour nor the vehicle startled me—she was a model. When I got into the car, it was so dark, all I could make out was a lot of hair, black fur and stillettos shrouded in a fog of Chanel No. 5.

She had a bottle of Stoli pressed to her lips like a pacifier and wouldn't say a word. It was hard to tell if she was simply pouting or trying to create an air of mystery. Could have been she was just drunk.

The limo raced downtown. The Rolling Stones' "Sympathy for the Devil" filled the silence. I thought that we were headed to a trendy bistro or a hot Soho nightspot. I looked up and we were about to get on the Brooklyn Bridge.

When I asked her where we were going, she suddenly started screaming in a language that I had never heard before and jumped out of the moving limo. Two cars swerved to miss her and rammed each other. She made a mad dash towards the railing and was grabbed just in time by me and the driver. It was pouring rain.

When the cops got there, she was babbling incoherently. They wanted information. All I knew was her first name. She had neither ID nor money on her. From the driver I found out that she had rented the limo in my name.

I said a relieved "au revoir" as the police hauled her off amidst the shouts of angry motorists. I then hopped in the front seat of the limo and got a slice of pizza with the driver. He was glad to be rid of her too.

Neither one of us ever heard from Arielle again, but I saw her recently on the cover of a French fashion magazine.

James Ellroy

©HOWARD ROSENBERG

Born in Los Angeles in 1948, James Ellroy is the author of eight critically acclaimed crime novels, including *The Black Dahlia* and *The Big Nowhere*, both national bestsellers.

It was a blind date, of course, and I was desperate: age twenty-one, big and geeky, six foot three, 140 pounds—forty of those pounds zits. The first woman I ever slept with turned gay shortly after our coupling. She moved in with another woman—and both of them were sick and tired of my snouting around them with triads in my mind. The year was 1969—and I couldn't have gotten laid in a whorehouse.

So the two women lovebirds set me up with the kid sister of a guy they shared office space with. Her name was Olivia. She was eighteen and a senior at a swanky girl's school in Los Angeles. She needed a date for the prom—I needed a date, period.

The prom required formal attire, I didn't own any. I borrowed a black suit from a short, fat buddy, oversized shoes from another pal. I bought a large tube of Clearasil to camouflage my pizza face and glommed a stick-shift '53 Buick that I couldn't drive too well. I looked like a cross between a crow on snowshoes and the "Before" in an ad for Stri-Dex Pads. I drove to Olivia's house—hot to trot.

My heart filled when Olivia opened the door.

Looks mean less to me now—probably because I'm forty-one

and married to a fox *and I was desperate then*. But one look at Olivia and I must have looked crestfallen.

Her face was as blank as pudding—vanilla. She was nearly as tall as I was and her shoulders were so narrow that her spaghetti straps kept slipping off. She wore no makeup, no jewelry except for a giant crucifix. Her first words were: "I don't usually go out with un-saved guys, but my brother said you were tall!" I did not want to engage in sexual intercourse with her—at the zenith of my sex drought which had lasted, with few hiatuses, from my birth in 1948 until the present.

We went to the prom.

I slid my pants down and cinched them with my necktie to hide the fact that the cuffs only extended to my ankles.

I went to the can and guzzled the bottle of Thunderbird wine I'd brought with me for savoir faire; Olivia didn't look so bad when I came back out. I started telling her lies about the size of my organ and how only a very tall girl like herself would be likely to accommodate me. She kept asking me if I was interested in being saved.

A guy I knew from high school breezed by and invited me to smoke a joint with him. We toked up in the parking lot. I was blasted and was now a heat-seeking missile aimed at females in general. My buddy told me who the certified dirty girls were, and to my astonishment Olivia was one of them—all I had to do was undergo a convincing and very rapid religious transformation!

Now, I grew up blandly Protestant—and I knew enough shtick to get me at least to first base. I went back to Olivia, lambasted her with scripture, the fact that I had my own pad, and reminded her of my immense size. Olivia was frightened—not impressed. She asked me to drive her home immediately. I burned the clutch out on the ride over. Two blocks from her house, Olivia got out and ran the rest of the way. I walked home, my phone rang. It was my high school pal, who said, "Gotcha! And I gotcha on tape! I recorded you groveling to that bowwow!"

He sent me the tape. I kept it as a memento of limbo: How low can you go? I put Olivia out of my mind, years passed.

In the fall of 1981 I got a phone call at home in New York. Olivia had read my first novel, thought she recognized herself as the love interest, and just happened to be in town. Would I like to come over to her hotel?

I went.

She had filled out nicely.

She still wore a crucifix—her new one was Day-Glo.

We made love like passionate cougars.

She gave me crabs.

Robert Englund

Although Robert Englund has appeared in numerous television productions and twenty motion pictures, he is probably best known for his portrayal of one of the world's most notorious screen menaces—Freddy Krueger, the deformed villain of the *Nightmare on Elm Street* series of films.

I'm from that generation that grew up with a hard-on for girls that looked like Cheryl Tiegs.

Holly, the new girl in eleventh grade, was exactly that type: she had classic Cheryl Tiegs bangs, ironed blonde hair, turned down eyes, a washboard stomach, and a retainer, which we all thought was very sexy. She dressed in coulotte, corduroy dresses with nasty dark nylons and nasty black-and-white patent leather shoes. That was the fad in 1965. The look was halfway between greaser-prostitute fantasy and bad surfer girl.

For some reason or other, my buddy Russ convinced me to ask "Cheryl Tiegs incarnate" out for a double date with him and his girlfriend. To my amazement she said yes. At the time, I thought she had heard that I was like a "surf God," but later I found out that her sister, who was in my drama classes, told her that I was like this wonderful actor and was very funny.

Before and after this date, I had sort of this blessed life. I was the sidekick to all the young surfing studs in Southern California, so I got lucky with all the great, original, witty, sidekick girls, who, in fact, were more sexually promiscuous and more fun than the so-called American beauty roses. But since I had the *first date* in the school with the "new rose," the pressure was really on me.

Wouldn't you know it? Between the time I asked Holly out and the day of the date, I grew one of the biggest zits of my adolescence, right between my eyes. That tumor was the size of a dime!

I tried everything to dry it out: I went surfing every day after school, I laid in the sun, I used Clearasil, I used witch hazel, I used baking soda. Nothing worked. It seemed like there were just more layers on this zit than an onion!

The night of the big date I was mortified. Everything else about me was great: I had no other zits, my hair was at its good length, I had a tan, my jeans were nice and faded, my madras shirt was nice and faded, but that pimple!

I borrowed flesh-colored Clearasil from Russ, and I made him *and* his girlfriend promise that they wouldn't look at my eyebrows or bring up the zit on the double date. They were just going to avoid it, *they promised*!

We go to pick up Holly in a classic, two-door Chevy Nomad, with curtains on the windows. I never understood why fathers let their daughters go out with boys in cars like that, but, anyway, Holly gets into the back seat with me. Russ and his girlfriend are in the front. As we drive away, my good friend Russ reaches over the backseat, pushes the heel of his hand between my eyes and goes "Dingdong, Avon calling."

I turned so red the zit probably didn't show for the rest of the night.

I was utterly humiliated. There were only four people in the car, but it felt like the whole school was watching.

I can't remember what movie we saw at the drive-in, but I know it took me a full double-feature just to find the confidence to put my arm around the back of the backseat of the Nomad.

It was definitely a scarred, horrible, and tragic worst date.

Bob Feller

In his legendary career, Baseball Hall-of-Famer Bob Feller won 266 games, struck out 2,581 batters, pitched three no-hitters and twelve one-hitters against sluggers like Joe DiMaggio, Ted Williams, and Hank Greenberg. A Cleveland Indian from 1936 to 1956, Feller still attends spring training with his team.

Bob Feller (left) and teammate Jeff Heath

My worst date was nothing compared to the one my roommate on the Cleveland Indians, Jeff Heath, had back before World War II at the Shoreham Hotel in Washington, D.C.

We were sitting around the lobby one afternoon before playing a night game out at Griffith Stadium and there was this very nice looking blonde young lady there. She was about five-five, weighed about a hundred and twenty-five. All the players were eyeing her, but Jeff was the only one that had the intestinal fortitude to make a pass.

He also had the best shot at her because he was built like a Greek god. He was a great lookin' fella, should've been a movie actor, but he was a very fine major league baseball player. He was a leftfielder, and a left-handed hitter, and had a great personality.

Anyway, Jeff fixed up a date with this young lady. He left her a ticket for the game, then took her to dinner and probably had a drink or two afterward, then they wound up in her room. As he told it, they got into somewhat of a simple romantic position and she was not quite cooperating.

First thing he knew, she threw him on the floor, got him into a headlock, a step-over toe-hold, kicked him in the rear end, and walked out of the room. The next day he picked up the morning paper and saw that she was a world champion woman wrestler who was defending her title that night in Washington, D.C.

Jeff thought this was the funniest thing that ever happened to him in his life; he couldn't wait to tell everybody on the ball club.

As far as I know, it was the first and last date he ever had with a champ.

David Frost

David Frost is one of the best-known television interviewers in the world. Among those he has interviewed are U.S. Presidents Nixon, Bush, Reagan, Carter and Ford, Indira Gandhi, the Shah of Iran, Robert F. Kennedy, Yassar Arafat, Woody Allen, Prince Charles, Tennessee Williams, Orson Welles, Harold Wilson and the Beatles.

On one of my trips to Australia in the early seventies when I was traveling without a female companion—"living off the land," to quote the characteristically Australian phrase—a friend of mine said he knew a marvelous girl whom I would love to meet. "She really *loves* European men," he told me.

As I was driving her to the restaurant, I realized the reason why she loved European men: she only spoke Spanish! And Spanish was a language the only word of which I knew was *mañana*—and this was not a problem for *mañana*, this was tonight's problem. Unfortunately, the restaurant was not a Mexican one, which might at least have given us a start. As the two of us sat there scarcely exchanging a word, the waiter looked at me pityingly: clearly we were just another married couple who had run out of things to say to each other, or an unmarried couple who had had the row to end all rows before coming out for the evening.

After an hour of pure purgatory, my so-called friend turned up at the restaurant with another girl in tow whom he introduced to me while greeting the Spanish girl surprisingly warmly. It turned out that *he* spoke Spanish and that the two of them were having an affair and had decided to play a practical joke on me to see how I coped with the emergency. I feared I failed the test! However, all was not entirely lost, because the new girl turned out to be absolutely terrific, and we warmed to each other very quickly. Soon we were speaking the same language in more senses than one.

But that's another story.

Sam Fuller

Sam Fuller is a film-maker, author and journalist. Writer-director of *Steel Helmet, White Dog, Shock Corridor, The Big Red One* and others, he recently completed two films, *Street of No Return* and *Tinkling*. Fuller has written six novels, including *Quint's World, The Dark Page* and *Crown of India,* and is currently writing a seventh.

My old pal Bill pumped my hand with a good old pat. He felt sorry for me.

"With guys three years and no girls?" Bill was in shock. "That's criminal!"

I knew Bill before he got to sit behind that big desk commanding a major studio. On his wall were Truman and Eisenhower. In a corner, FDR. On a table three Oscars and an autographed picture of Lassie.

"Goddam it!" he barked like a good samaritan, "I've got to fix you up with a date tonight!"

I remembered a rifleman playing with himself in the North African shock tent after losing both his hands. That kind of determination was Bill's style.

But I had to deflate him. "No thanks, Bill. Not interested."

Bill's jaw dropped. He groaned. "Did you get hit in the balls?"

I grinned. "Hell, no, Bill... but below the equator I'll make my own choice... You know, before I shipped overseas, my first, and only blind date was a nightmare."

He understood and was sad about it. "Who arranged it?"

"My sergeant."

"I didn't know the army fixed you guys up with chicks."

"The infantry manual doesn't list pimping."

"Pimping?" He was having a stroke. "I'm talking about a nice, clean-cut, gorgeous doll named Aggie!"

"Does she like uniforms?"

"Maybe she hates them."

"That would be un-American!"

That night in the apartment house hallway across from the studio I heard "Roll Out the Barrel" pecked on a keyboard. Bill knocked. She opened the door. The music was coming from her apartment.

"Glad to meet you, corporal. I'm Aggie."

She kissed me on the mouth.

That expression going for a girl "hook, line and sinker" had always grated on me, but now I understood it wasn't really that corny. Eyeball to eyeball, Aggie and I knew that this was destiny. My adrenal glands were in overdrive. So were hers. I stared at her cleavage and saw Robespierre's head chopped off by the guillotine.

"We're shooting a whacky comedy about Marie Antoinette called *Let 'em Eat Cake!*" said Aggie. "I play Cherry Bang, one of her virgin go-betweens. No dialogue. I've been a starlet at Bill's studio for two years and still he won't give me any dialogue." She looked behind her and shouted. "The corporal's here!"

The piano stopped playing. A squad of beautiful starlets in different costumes from pictures they were up for, or in, or that had been made, charged me with hugs and kisses and made me sip champagne from their glasses. As Bill introduced each one, he grinned at me to prove that his credibility as a date-maker was intact.

They made a big fuss over me.

Aggie jockeyed me into the kitchen where Cleopatra and Annie Oakley were standing on the stove and toasting me a welcome while the Queen of Sheba was sitting atop the Frigidaire throwing me a kiss.

Then Aggie pulled me out and into the bedroom where Mata Hari and Gilda Gray were outshimmying each other in a wardrobe held together by paper clips.

I was drinking on an empty stomach so they escorted me back into the living room. The surprise spread was for a king. Each beauty offered: "Danish salmon, corporal!... Beluga caviar, corporal!... French foie gras, corporal!"

They fed me. Blondes, brunettes, redheads, long hair, short hair... and by the second bottle I went through they promoted me to general but never mentioned the war or asked for war stories... They were asked to make sure I had a good time... and they knew how.

Wrapped up in my harem, I tried to hang onto Aggie, but her face became their faces and I was climbing the candy mountain and dancing on the ceiling and never knowing which candy to pick, and the last thing I remembered was Theda Bara the Vamp in a transparent body stocking leading them all singing "These Foolish Things."

In the morning they were gone. I was alone with Bill.

"When I fix a date," he boasted, "it's a production. How'd you like Aggie?"

"Which one was Aggie?"

"You didn't score?"

"No."

"That's bad."

"If all dates turn out like that one, Bill, who wants a good date?"

Frank and Kathie Lee Gifford

Football Hall-of-Famer and Emmy Award-winning sportscaster Frank Gifford has been a member of the ABC NFL *Monday Night Football* broadcast team for nineteen years. He has also hosted several other ABC sports programs.

At one point a substitute anchor and special correspondent for *Good Morning America* while simultaneously co-hosting *Live with Regis & Kathie Lee*, Kathie Lee Gifford is now concentrating on the latter program. In 1988, she co-hosted the Winter Olympics for ABC with her husband, Frank.

He thought I had no taste.

She was going out with the wrong people.

He would set me up with these men who'd seen me on TV or he thought would be good for me.

I felt *my* friends would be much better for her.

They might have been. But every time *he* introduced me to them, no sparks flew.

She'd spend the whole time talking to me.

That's because I didn't like blind dates and would always have Frank come along to make things more comfortable.

The big brother.

Well, we were good friends on *Good Morning America* for about four years.

And she was *always* telling me about breaking up with somebody or something.

There weren't that many! I'd been dating this one guy for about a year when I got a call from this couple my boyfriend and I were planning to have brunch with that Sunday. They said, "Do you mind if we bring along a friend who has *nothing to do?*"

I was *playing tennis* with the husband.

They told me it was Frank and I said, "That's great. I love Frank Gifford." So the five of us had a lovely Sunday brunch at Mortimers.

It wasn't lovely. Her date preferred to work the room for business contacts rather than pay attention to Kathie. I've seen a lot of those types in my life and they have their priorities...

A woman is a trophy to them, not a person.

So as we walked out the door, I said to Kathie, "You're not going to marry that jerk, are you?"

I said snidely, "Well, I might."

Well, you were dying to marry him, let's put it that way.

This will lead to divorce. I *wasn't* dying to marry him.

Come on, Kath...

One night, about a year later, a bulletin from heaven flashed in my head, "Quit crying the blues and change your life," it said. "If you settle for what you have, you deserve what you get." So I broke up with this man and just happened to have a lunch date scheduled with Frank the next day.

The camp counselor.

He was.

I said, "Kathie, you need to get out of the traffic. My divorce is imminent. I haven't really been going out with anybody. Why don't we just hang out together a little bit?" I honestly never thought anything would develop.

That's what they all say.

It was gradual—

Five months later, we got married!

I treated her right.

That's a real aphrodisiac.

That's what they all say.

Seriously, it took somebody like Frank to help me see what a bad date I'd been on at Mortimers.

And what a good date could be.

Alan Ginsberg

ROBERT FRANK

Alan Ginsberg is an acclaimed poet, political and gay rights activist and photographer. He became known to the general public as part of the "Beat Generation" or "San Francisco Renaissance" in 1955. In addition to *Howl*, he has published fifteen books of poetry and twelve books of prose.

When I was horny in my early twenties, I went up to a gay bar on 72nd Street, West Side. I'd never been there before, and have never been there since.

The place was very nondescript. A normal mix of rough trade and hustlers, old queens and young queers, young gay people and a little older gay people.

I hung around and I noticed this big, young guy at the bar. He had a nice-looking face. The body wasn't that interesting. But there was a kind of magnetism to him at first sight in the dim light of the bar.

We both got a little drunk and I wound up following him out. With all the noise, I didn't actually get any chance to have a conversation until we got outside and he said, "Come home with me, but I don't wanna do anything now, okay? Come home."

I found this a little confusing. He was hanging around in a gay bar and did invite me home. Then again, I had just been through a long period of not sleeping with anyone and was forcing myself to go out and make some kind of human contact. Perhaps I got my signals mixed up.

He led me to his furnished room, the kind you could get in those days for seven or ten dollars a week.

We finally wound up in bed naked, or at least with his drawers down and mine down. I started making love to him and he kept saying, "Oh, no, don't do that. Don't, don't," while he kept his erection for maybe half an hour. Finally he came. Then he got angry at me for making him come. Absolutely furious. It was like date rape, but I don't know who was raping whom.

I found out a week later I had crabs.

This was perhaps thirty-five or forty years ago, but it still sticks in my mind as being one of the most quizzical and in some respects the most unpleasant encounters I have ever had. I felt dirty and demeaned. I'd demeaned him and demeaned myself. It's a very, very rare situation. I usually have the most pleasant memories of the people I've slept with over the years. And still have many friendships among those I've romanced. That night, however, I felt ashamed of myself that I'd been so horny I kinda forced the issue and ignored his protesting. Then again, he was protesting naked, in *his* bed, in *his* house, with crabs.

Whoopi Goldberg

© 1990 MICHAEL JACOBS/MIP

The same year Whoopi Goldberg won a Golden Globe for her role in *The Color Purple*, she won a Grammy Award for the record album of her startling one-woman Broadway show. Since then, Whoopi has starred in films such as *Jumpin' Jack Flash*, *Fatal Beauty*, *Clara's Heart* and *Homer and Eddie*.

My worst date?
The day Kennedy died, the New York City blackout and 1955.

Al Goldstein

Publisher of *Screw* magazine. Al Goldstein produces his own outrageous cable-TV show called *Midnight Blue* and a newsletter for grown-up kids called "Gadget."

One year I spent probably $50,000 on dating: I had an ad in a New York magazine for a year. Cost me about $20,000. I put an ad for one year in an L.A. magazine. I put another in one of the monthlies, another in one of the weeklies. I joined two video dating services, one in New York called Video Resources, and one in L.A. called Great Expectations. As if that weren't enough, I also signed up for a matchmaking service called The Godmothers, where you pay $1,000 and they give you ten names.

Through The Godmothers, I met a perky, thirty-eight-year-old brunette named Camille. We went out a few times. I wouldn't say we were in love, but she was a bright, fun lady who, like me, was also in the middle of a hellish divorce.

On our third date, Camille said if I needed any money, she could help me. I never had a woman offer me money before, so I said jokingly, "How much are we talking about?" She said, "$50,000."

Fifty thousand dollars? I don't know many people in normal life who have $50,000 available to loan someone!

Later that night, we came back to my place, and I noticed one of her two sons, sitting in a car parked in front of my house with the motor running. This son was nineteen years old and he was *not* at all delicate.

I thought that was a little strange, but I didn't think too much more about it until I got a call from D.B., one of my Italian distributors, who'd been with *Screw* since its inception twenty-one years ago. D.B. couldn't talk to me on the phone, he said; we had to meet.

"What's the story with your dating Camille?" D.B. demanded gruffly.

"I met her through a dating service," I replied casually.

"Well, okay, at least you've got a defense."

"Do I need one?!" I asked in surprise.

It turned out that Camille's husband did ten years for extortion and was a good friend of John Gotti, a reputed Mafia boss in New York City. Like many Mafia guys, Camille's husband operated with a double standard: even though he had this blonde bimbo girlfriend stashed at a midtown hotel, he did not want his wife, who he was separated from, to see anybody. His Italian macho image was at stake.

"Al, we have to have the truth reach these people," D.B. said, "because they wanna kill you."

I couldn't believe it. My whole life has been surrounded with controversies, but the first time I'm in real physical danger, I'm innocent!

That's exactly what D.B. intended to tell Gotti and his friends when he had, as he put it, "a sit-down" with them. He said it was necessary because there was an actual contract on me and he was concerned. I would have loved to have known that I was a high ticket payoff, but I have the feeling I was only a $5,000 pop.

First thing I did, I took my bulletproof vest out of dry cleaning. Then I stopped talking to Camille. This made her nuts. She kept calling and begging to see me and I kept saying, "Look, I don't intend to die right now for you. Wait till D.B. talks to John."

I didn't hear anything from D.B. for a couple of weeks, during which time I got more and more nervous. I started to walk in and out of my house at odd times, always looking in all directions.

When I was in my car, I felt better, because I had this Chinese chauffeur who was an ex-New York City police officer and was armed, but I wasn't exactly sleeping well at nights, and my divorce battles weren't making things any easier.

Then I got calls from other friends who were associated with these people who said, "This is a bad person that is after you." And when *these people* say somebody is a *bad person*, you've *gotta believe* it's a bad person. The more pieces I had of the whole picture, the more terrifying it seemed.

Soon after that, I got another panicked call from Camille. She wanted me to tell D.B. to tell John Gotti that I picked her up at a bar. If I didn't say that, she feared her husband would kill her too. I said, "If he doesn't kill you, he'll kill me. I have to tell the truth about The Godmothers."

I don't know if Camille is alive, because I've never heard from her again. That would be a shame 'cause she was a nice lady.

A few weeks later, D.B. called and indicated that I should be okay, that he had put his personal prestige on the line. I'm eternally indebted to him, although there is nothing I can do about it, now that he's dead. He disappeared two years ago, and as far as I know, he's never been found.

Looking back, it would figure that a dating service called The Godmothers would produce a woman with Mafia connections.

Stephen Jay Gould

A lecturer at Harvard University, paleontologist Stephen Jay Gould has received twenty-five honorary degrees, a MacArthur "genius" grant, and countless other academic awards. His latest book is *Wonderful Life: The Burgess Shale and the Nature of History.*

HARVARD NEWS SERVICE

Everyone has stories about bad dates with sexual partners, and there are many lovely women I could tell you about. But they're all alive. So I'm going to construe the notion of date broadly to mean: any arranged meeting, for a particular purpose, with another person of some importance to one's life, and tell you a two-part story of college recruitment.

My high school record wasn't outstanding, but I think it was good enough to gain admission to Oberlin College in Ohio. Where I really flubbed was in my personal interview, which was an unmitigated disaster for the following reason. That was my worst date, my meeting with this man.

He was an Oberlin alumnus. He was a young, hotshot, beginning businessman in New York City. The technique he used, I'm absolutely certain, *was not* condoned by Oberlin College, but was his own invention, based on some snappy notion of corporate toughness.

I was not quite sixteen years old at the time, having graduated early from high school, and I was very nervous. Very insecure, very ill at ease. Knowing me now, of course, you would never think that. But back then...

I walked in, I sat down, I looked at this hotshot beginning businessman and I saw that his fly was all the way open.

I didn't know what to do. Do you tell the man, do you not?

I decided to keep quiet and spent the first half of the interview absolutely flubbing every question—looking up at the ceiling, looking down at the floor, looking everywhere but at his gaping fly.

About midway through the interview, in a sort of mechanical way that made me know—even though I'm not that perceptive of a person—that made me know absolutely immediately this was a trick, that he'd done it on purpose, that it was his way of testing someone for equipoise or for maturity, he looked down and he said stiffly, "Oh, dear, MY FLY is open," and zipped it back up. I was so mad at this technique I flubbed the rest of the interview.

Needless to say, I didn't get in to Oberlin. And although I can't prove it, I do think it was due to my performance at the personal interview. Now that, in itself, is my worst date. But I wouldn't even bother telling you this story (because it wouldn't be significant enough) if there weren't a sequel. And the sequel is as follows:

I went to Antioch, and then I went to Columbia and got my Ph.D., and was invited up to Harvard, where I've been for the past twenty years, for an interview. The interviewer was a man who later became my dear colleague, Bernie Kummel. He was the senior paleontologist. It was his job to interview new people.

Once again, I was quite nervous. The first morning I arrived in Cambridge, I went to a class of Bernie Kummel's. Afterwards, we went up for a cup of coffee, and, after that, to the men's room. We came back down to his office, sat down at his desk and were about to start what was going to be the first interview when I noticed that *his fly was open.*

Oh, no, I thought, here we go again.

But I wasn't going to be fooled a second time. I looked Kummel straight in the eye and said, "Dr. Kummel, excuse me, but your fly is open."

He took one look down and said, "Whoops!" which made it perfectly obvious it was an accident. I then told him the Oberlin story, which he thought was enormously funny, and we proceeded to have a delightful conversation. It was the greatest icebreaker.

So I think in retrospect, I was hired at Harvard because I knew what to do, thanks to the first bad date. That's my story. A bad date rectified.

Spalding Gray and Renée Shafransky

Spalding Gray is a writer, actor and performer who has created eleven auto-biographical mono-logues, including his acclaimed *Swimming to Cambodia* and *Sex and Death to the Age of 14.* His novel, *Impossible Vacation*, will be published by Alfred Knopf in the fall of 1990.

Formerly a journalist and film curator, Renée Shafransky is now a screenwriter and pro-ducer. She produced the film *Swimming to Cambodia*. Her latest screenplay, *Death and Taxes*, is being directed by Harold Ramis for Universal Pictures.

Spalding's story:

You know who I dated most when I was in boarding school and college? My mother. I had an almost classical oedipal relationship with her.

We'd go to see Bergman films and discuss them afterwards. Go see *Ben Hur* because she was very religious. Go see *Tom Jones* and she'd get very upset because, "How could a scoundrel get away with that?" We'd have discussions like that. So there was no room, or I didn't allow it, or there was some sort of guilt in there, but there was no room for a lot of dates.

I guess the first real date I went on was with Renée, the woman I now live with, and that was when I was thirty-seven or thirty-eight years old.

I was in this twelve year relationship with a woman that I met when I was acting at a small theater in Saratoga, New York, and she was going to Skidmore College. It was back in 1964-1965, and that twelve year relationship was starting to come apart because my girlfriend and I worked together. And when the work began to end, the relationship began to come apart. This was around the time of a big awards dinner.

The *Soho News* was giving me an award for best performance in the play that my girlfriend of twelve years had directed. The awards ceremony and the party afterwards were at Studio 54. I'd never been to Studio 54 and I was really excited about having a look at it.

They really treated us like shit, those fascistic Studio 54 guards. They made us line up in the back with the invitations that had been mailed to us in hand. I had forgotten mine. And I almost didn't get in until a couple in front of me got so angry and shouted, "Don't you know who you're talking to? That's Spalding Gray! He won one of those awards tonight. This party is for him!" And they just took their invitations, and gave them to me and said "Shove it!" and walked out.

Studio 54. Everyone was dancing on the floor. All the downtown art scene. I was dancing with different people. And moving around the space and partying up and having a good time. And I looked across the crowded room (it was just like that) and I saw Renée's face. I had no idea who she was. But what struck me was the absolute openness in her face, the devilishness, the jolliness. The "Hey, you'd be a mensch if you could take me on." Lots of different things going on. Lots of different things in a way that I didn't see anywhere else on the whole floor. Because usually, if I'm going after an object, I go after bodies. That's not what struck me about Renée at all, at first. It was the gamine-ness, the fun in her face. The absolute feisty delight.

I asked her to dance. I was very used to doing what I would call "art dancing" and then "contact," so it was not unusual for me to make body contact while I was dancing. She felt, later I found out, that I was really coming on very fast by pressing against her with my "contact."

I think we had one or two dances. It was rather clumsy. Nothing special about it. There was no great chemistry going on. And then she fled like Cinderella. I think she even left her pocketbook behind.

She told me later that she fled because she saw me there with my ex, assumed I was a married man, and wasn't going to get involved. She didn't know that I wasn't married, and we were breaking up, myself and my previous girlfriend.

While we were dancing, I remember she told me that she worked as a programmer at an experimental theater. There were only two that I knew of: The Film Forum and The Collective on White Street, so I tracked her down to White Street. I went down there, very formally, went to her back office there, and asked her out on a date, I think, for that night. She was very surprised to see me.

We went to Mickey's, a pool bar down in lower Manhattan, which was later bought by John Belushi. She was very nervous. I don't even remember how I was feeling. Again, I think I was still going through shock. I went through it for years, breaking up from that twelve year relationship.

I remember that we had some drinks. We played some pool. She's a great pool player. And then I don't know if we made the agreement there, that we were going back to her place, or whether I just walked her back and she invited me up. She was living on John Street in a converted office with a small bathtub in it. I just thought the whole idea of it was very romantic.

We went up to her place and it's all kind of amnesia to me how it led to us getting into bed. I mean, in those days it wasn't a big issue. But *today*, things have *really* changed.

Anyway, somewhere right at the beginning of making love, she said "Excuse me, but I think I'm going to throw up." I didn't take it personally. I politely got off from on top of her and let her go down the hall to the bathroom.

She might remember it differently, but I think I went to see if she was all right and then we came back to bed and went to sleep. We may have made love in the morning. And although I have real sexual amnesia for that particular night and the next morning, I assume we had good sex. Because we did early on in the relationship and still do. The throwing up, in fact, was delightful. It bonded us. It gave a sense of humor and a humaneness to the whole thing. It's like getting to know someone very quickly in a very intimate way. And Renée was very impressed that I would be able to go through that and not be repulsed by it.

That was the big date of my life. Studio 54. Almost didn't get in. I was thirty-seven, maybe thirty-eight years old and I felt like a kid.

Renée's story:

It was 1976 and I was standing outside Studio 54 waiting on line to cover the *Soho News* Drama Awards for a tiny New York City paper called *The Villager*. This cute actor walked by and was let in first because he was "the talent" getting the award.

The woman journalist next to me remarked, "Oh, that's Spalding Gray. Isn't he cute." "Yes, he's cute." I quipped, "But he lives with somebody." (A friend of mine had told me that, after I told him I was convinced Spalding was staring at me throughout the performance of his one-man show, *Sex and Death to the Age of 14*.)

We went inside Studio 54 and it was packed. Spalding, I noticed, was spending most of the evening talking to this woman, who I assumed was the woman he lived with. I spent my time standing on the edge of the dance floor.

At some point, someone tapped me on the shoulder. I turned around and it was Spalding. "Do you want to dance?" he asked. I was very surprised and thought, Okay. The woman he lives with is only a few feet away, this is going to be interesting.

We started dancing, and at the end of the first song he just kept on dancing. By the fourth song, the only way I can describe it is, he started *touching me* while we were dancing. Now *he* would insist that this is perfectly normal. Where I come from, you *don't touch* someone you haven't even been introduced to yet. I thought, this is too weird. He must be bombed. Besides, he's supposed to live with somebody. No matter how cute I think he is, *no way*!

At the end of the sixth song I said to him, "I'm gonna go get a drink. I'll be right back." And I left. I thought if I stayed there any longer I'd get into a situation that wouldn't be any good.

On Sunday (which was a few days later), for some weird reason, I went to pick up the mail at my other place of business, a film theater in lower Manhattan. I heard this noise behind me and I turned around and, again, it was Spalding. This time he was standing at the door with a little envelope in his hand. "I was just going to leave you a note," he said.

"How did you find me?"

"Your friend."

The same friend who told me he lives with somebody. That's interesting.

I opened the note and it said something leaden like, "Something was started that we should finish. What is your phone number? Let's go on a date."

Now at that time, I was in what I would call my "hyper-feminist" period, so I didn't trust him for several reasons: a) I heard he lived with somebody, b) the way he danced with me, and c) the word date was not in my vocabulary yet. This was 1976 and I was not used to going on formal dates.

But at any rate I said, "Come inside. Why don't we talk for a while." I sat behind my big desk because I ran the place. He sat on the other side of it, like an interview, and I essentially interviewed him like a shrink interviewing a patient.

"Well, I've heard you live with somebody. And that you're in a relationship."

"Well, uhmm, it's sort of an open-ended relationship."

"What does that mean?"

"It might be ending. It might be open."

"Oh, that sounds great," I said sarcastically.

He stood up. "I guess this wasn't a very good idea."

"No, wait a second, you asked me on a date. You can't take that back."

We arranged to meet a few days later at a local bar where you play pool. A friend of Spalding's was there too, so the three of us sat around having drinks and playing pool. And, yes, that was the night that we went back to my place.

I was, at that time, living in an office building, and when we got there I asked Spalding, a little nervously, if he'd like to come upstairs. He said yes.

We sat around. He had a brandy. I had a brandy. Then, I have no memory of how, we fell into bed together. As soon as we did, I began to realize that the room was spinning, and that, in fact, I was going to be very sick.

I thought, My God, Renée, you really have no choice here. You're going to have to say to this guy, Cut it out, I'm going to throw up. Instead I said, "Stop!"

"Why?" he asked breathlessly and in shock. I guess he thought I was going to have some moral objection, like "No. We've only just met." I said, "I'm going to be very sick." And he started laughing.

He spent much of the evening nursing me, which I contend is the entire reason that we have been in a relationship for nine years. Because while he was nursing me I thought, Oh, this is interesting. He's a great nurse. He has a sense of humor. He didn't walk out and say you're disgusting. He just nursed—which is much more in depth than what you normally get when you're having a one-night stand.

In the morning, he hung around, we had breakfast, then he went off to Baltimore on a train. And for the next two years, we had a very stormy breakup, back together, breakup, back together relationship: three months on, two months off, four months on, one month off.

I think it's what you call "Rebound." I was "the rebound." But somehow, because of the throwing up, I was the rebound that stuck.

Bob Greene

KAREN P. PULFER

A syndicated columnist, Bob Greene appears in more than 200 newspapers throughout the U.S. He is the author of nine books, two of which are bestsellers. He is a contributing correspondent for *ABC News Nightline* and a contributing editor to *Esquire* magazine.

When I was a senior in high school, I managed to get a date with one of the most beautiful girls in our part of Ohio. This was the kind of impossibly perfect blonde goddess you only see in movies about California surfers—but against all the odds, she actually walked the hallways of our school.

I could hardly believe it when she said yes to me—she was actually going to spend a Saturday night on a date with me, when she could have had her choice of the football quarterback, the captain of the basketball team, or any other guy in the school. I wanted to impress her, so I took her to the most popular movie of the moment—*Mary Poppins*.

Which is where the trouble came in. All the way to the theater, she kept referring to the movie as "Mary Popkins." You have to understand—no one in America was unaware of the title *Mary Poppins*. But in the car, it was "Mary Popkins" every time it left her mouth. I figured that once we got to the theater, she would understand the error of her ways. All during the movie, though, when she would whisper something to me, she referred to what we were watching as "Mary Popkins." And on the way home, it was—without variation—"Mary Popkins."

Certainly this was no sin. And even though it began to have the same effect as a fingernail scraping across a chalkboard, she was so physically lovely that I am sure I would have forgiven her each and every "Mary Popkins" if she had shown a glimmer of genuine interest in me. She didn't, though; I was just a filler on an inexplicably unbooked Saturday night for her, and each reference to "Mary Popkins" was merely more evidence of how little the evening meant to her.

I have no idea where she is today. But with the current craze for movie sequels, she is never far from the back of my consciousness. One of these days some West Coast producer is bound to cash in on the financial possibilities of a follow-up to that movie—and when it hits the theaters, there is no way in the world I will be able to think of it as anything but "Mary Popkins II."

Herbie Hancock

CORY GRAVES

Herbie Hancock has led or collaborated on nearly fifty records, running the gamut from work with Miles Davis to funk jazz. The multiple award-winning composer-performer won an Oscar and a Grammy for his score to *Round Midnight.* Other scores include Antonioni's *Blow-Up* and Dennis Hopper's *Colors.*

This is a story about those "three little words"—"I love you."

I always thought that saying "I love you" was something important. I never would say that to a girl who I was dating, just to say it. In fact, I generally never said it at all, thinking that I would only say it to the girl I would marry.

In 1961, I was working with Donald Byrd and it involved going to New York for a few weeks, and then to Chicago, my hometown. When I was growing up there, one of my mom's close friends had a daughter a few years younger than I was. Basically, as kids, we knew each other from a distance.

So, years later, when I came to Chicago with Donald, for some reason, I was feeling pretty miserable. I'm not sure why. And I'm not exactly sure how, but this girl from my childhood and I remet after I had been in Chicago a couple of weeks. It changed my state of mind completely. I couldn't believe how much I liked her. And it was so funny because I'd known her before—all my life, really, but, in fact, hadn't known her at all.

She was very special. We had a great time and we started seeing each other a lot.

One night, after we'd been together for a few weeks, I brought her home. There we were at the front door. We started kissing good night, and I just felt so close to her. I really cared for her.

As we stood there, holding each other, she whispered in my ear, "Herbie, I love you so much," and I heard myself answering, "I like you so much, too."

Maybe it was just a habit by then, being too shy I guess, about saying "I love you" to a girl. And I was crazy about this particular person. But something in me still couldn't say it.

This did not pass her by. She pulled away from me, furious, and never spoke to me again.

All this took place in the summer of 1961. And I left Chicago soon after that.

About six months later, I was in New York again. On New Year's Eve, I found myself riding the subway, going back to the Bronx where I was staying. It was just past midnight, and all these people on the train were joking and kissing each other. I saw couples sitting together, holding hands and hugging each other. I sat by myself, watching so many happy people and I don't think I ever felt quite as lonely in my life.

When I got home, I picked up the phone and called that girl in Chicago. I told her I missed her and felt so terrible about what had happened. I apologized to her, and was so upset, I started crying. She was pretty nice about it, but she would never completely forgive me.

Eventually, we saw each other again and continued to be friends. But that romance died on that summer night when I didn't say "I love you."

Gregory Hines

GREG GORMAN

When Gregory Hines was almost three years old, he began tap dancing with his big brother Maurice. At five, the brothers went pro. At eighteen, Dad joined the act. On Broadway, Gregory earned three Tony nominations for *Eubie, Comin' Uptown,* and *Sophisticated Ladies.* In film he has starred in *Tap, White Nights, Running Scared, The Cotton Club* and *Wolfen.*

I had dropped out of dancing and was living in Venice, California, like a hippie, single parent. I was already involved with the woman I'm married to now, but in '74, people who were going out together were also seeing other people. It seems like such a weird thought nowadays, but it was the tail end of the sexual revolution and that was the way it was.

At the time, I was playing guitar and singing with a jazz rock band called "Severance." We were touring the local beer bars along the beach, so I had a pretty high visibility situation in the community.

One night I met this woman named Ramona at a club called the Come Back Inn. She was about my height. She had a very interesting nose, large breasts, and was just a very attractive and very shapely lady. We got into a conversation and she invited me over for dinner the next night. Usually, in those days, if I met somebody at a bar, we'd "get down'" that night. That's why her invitation turned me on so much. It was refreshing.

The moment I stepped into her apartment the next evening, I realized I was in a terrible situation. She had cats.

I'm allergic to cats, *very intensely* allergic to cats. When I come into a house, no matter how large the house is, if there's a cat in there, I know immediately—unless the people have the house so well kept and so well ventilated they've flushed out all the hairs.

Now, if I go into a house and there's a cat, I can say right away, "I gotta go, I'm sorry, I'm allergic to cats." But in those days, I was on some kind of macho-denial trip that was certainly made a little worse that evening because Ramona looked so beautiful and so sexy. I could feel the tension mounting.

On top of it, she had the place all romantic: she had the table set up with lit candles. She had a couple more candles around the room and she also had incense burning.

I thought to myself, Gregory, you're just gonna zen this thing out. You're not gonna stop breathing like you normally do. You're gonna walk in and not say anything about the problem.

Well, next thing I discover, Ramona's serving cheese fondue—which gives me the most heavy mucus—and she has this evening planned. We aren't gonna just sit down and eat real fast, we're going to spend some time hanging out with these cats!

We sit down on the couch and she pulls out these photo albums she wants me to see. One cat naturally sits on my lap. She said, "Oh, that's Wilbur, isn't he beautiful?" I don't find cats attractive. No matter how beautiful a cat is, when I look at it, it looks to me like a piece of phlem.

She was a belly dancer, so she shows me pictures of that. She also worked with child care and shows me pictures of that, too. She made jewelry and displays it for me. She had a varied past. Interesting woman. Interesting conversation. It had all the makings of a great evening, except for Wilbur.

Within an hour, Wilbur starts to do his stuff. I can feel I—I—I—I'm almost in trouble. My words are coming out short. I don't have much air to expel. She's saying, "What do you think of that picture?" Half-hour earlier, I was saying, "Oh, that's nice," now I'm saying "Oh, i—hi—."

Finally she says, "Let's eat."

We open the wine I'd brought. Drinking it doesn't help. Midway through dinner my shoulders are hunched up to my neck and I'm gasping for little pieces of air. Three quarters of the way through dinner, I just cannot breathe anymore. Finally, it's clear I have to go.

"I—I"

"What," she asks, quite concerned, "Is something wrong with dinner?"

I shake my head no and stand up.

"No— go—od..."

Now I'm getting to the point now where I can only say one word at a time. I can't put a sentence together.

"Cats," I get out.

"What about the cats?

"Air." Now I'm at the door, I'm leaning out, trying to breath. "Air," I repeat with difficulty.

As soon as Ramona understands me, she gets offended. "Why didn't you tell me when you first walked in the door?"

I couldn't even get out the words, "I'm sorry I should've," or "See you tomorrow." "Tomorrow" was out of the question. Literally, all I could squeeze out was, "Bye."

It took me two days to recover. I had to sleep that night with my head up and the next day I had nothing but mint tea.

Two weeks later, I bumped into Ramona again on the beach. "Feeling better?" she inquired rather coolly.

I apologized and told her I should have said something about the cats as soon as I saw Wilbur. She said it was all right. But it wasn't, really. It was a very awkward situation. Had I called her the next day, maybe we could've still gotten together, but I was too embarrassed and humiliated to even try.

I definitely missed a great night: beautiful woman and all the potential in the world for a terrific evening, but it turned out to be a bad date.

Abbie Hoffman

A former pharmaceuticals salesman, Abbie Hoffman became an antiwar activist and revolutionary whose ever-quotable style made him a media celebrity and best-selling author. A founder of the Youth International Party or Yippies, Hoffman continued his activism and political organizing until his death. At one point, he was a member of the FBI's 10 Most Wanted List.

I made love to a woman and she pulled a gun out. It wasn't personal. She said she needed it to get onto the freeway. That was kind of average. An average date.

My worst date, however, was the date I had to disappear. That was early in February of 1974. I had essentially been planning probably the most difficult odyssey of my life. I had been building an underground network that was international. I had been preparing for plastic surgery, getting crucial documents, learning where I would change my hairstyle and my gait. All this was necessary because the FBI is a headline-hunting organization and since those boys and their CIA buddies had already amassed over 70,000 files on me, why would they stop?

I couldn't exactly have a going-away party because that would have been considered bail violation. Instead, my wife and I made love for days. Then I got very close to the kid. Because I thought I would never come back. Ever. In fact, I was determined if they caught me, I would be taken in dead.

The day I left, it was snowing, I remember. My wife drove me to the airport in our car. We got a flat tire in the middle of New York City. Police wanted to know if they could help... we thought that was a kind of a bad start.

Then I flew to Richmond, Virginia, where I gave a speech that I ended with, "If Rockefeller comes looking for me, tell him I went thataway." I pointed north because I was headed south, since the most interesting blacks at the time were living in Atlanta. Hair straightening was a big fashion. So I got my kinky hair straightened and turned into a blond in Atlanta.

Then I bought a set of very different kind of clothes and flew cross-country to Los Angeles, where I had plastic surgery without the doctor knowing who I was. Great nose. Of my six noses, that nose was the prettiest. It's not the one I have now. Gravity has its way...

In Los Angeles, I enrolled in a Spanish course to change my Boston accent and a karate course to change my gait. Immediately lost fifteen pounds. After about three weeks in hiding, I disappeared into the jungles of Mexico. And it was there that I was officially declared a fugitive.

My father died a few weeks after I vanished. Two hundred FBI agents paid their respects at the funeral, which wasn't surprising. They'd already forced customers away from his business, trying to stop me, after they failed with every other government trick you could imagine—including dope frames and broken noses, courtesy of White House thugs. It's a tough job changing people's minds.

Later in this life, I was able to become extremely mobile and visible, to the extent that "as another person" I was testifying in Congress, leading grass-roots campaigns, speaking at universities, appearing on television, while "as Abbie," I was seeing my kids, doing TV interviews here and in other countries, publishing books, calling radio stations through complicated means, defying the police to try to chase me. Little things.

After many years, people like me realized that we could come back and be ourselves. And when we did... WOW!

Henry Jaglom

SUSAN SCHACTER

Henry Jaglom's films as a writer-director include *A Safe Place, Tracks, Sitting Ducks, Can She Bake a Cherry Pie?* *Always, Someone to Love,* and *New Year's Day.* Jaglom created the Women's Film Company, a venture which produces films by women directors.

She looked beautiful when she walked out the door of her parents' apartment. Her chestnut brown hair was swept up and pinned very high on her head. She was wearing this great, gray, silk dress, with little Cuban heels, a string of baby pearls, a hint of pink lipstick and white gloves. That's the part that I couldn't get over, the white gloves.

Then again, I didn't know what to expect. I had gone to parties and necked a little, but I had never gone out on a date with this fifteen-year-old daughter of a friend of my parents or anyone else for that matter. This was very nervous making. I figured we'd probably end up kissing a little bit after the movies, but I didn't know what to say to her as we drove downtown in the taxi. "I think it's going to be a good movie," I tried, "Brando's in it... I'm also an actor." She was very sweet and answered, "Yes, and Uh-huh" at all the right places.

When we got to Times Square, I jumped out of the taxi, paid the driver the fare, which I remember was *exactly one dollar, one* quarter and *one* dime, walked over to the ticket counter, bought the tickets, and turned to say to my date, "Oh, it really looks like it's gonna be good," but she wasn't there.

I looked around in panic and couldn't see her anywhere. Oh, god, I thought, somehow I've lost her in Times Square! What are you supposed to do if you lose a fifteen-year-old girl in Times Square and you're all of sixteen?

I quickly scanned the area again and noticed that the taxi we came in hadn't moved. In fact, my date was sitting there in the backseat, with the door that I had left open knocking against the curb. In the front seat, the taxi driver was looking very, very irritated.

As I ran over to the cab, I suddenly thought, she hasn't moved because she's sick. I didn't know what to do with a girl on the first date. I *really* didn't know what to do with a *sick* date!! So I asked, in a very concerned voice, "What's the matter? What's the matter?" She answered, without losing a beat, as if she had been doing this all her life, "*All* the young men who have *ever* taken me out have *helped* me out of taxicabs."

How many could that have been? She was a fifteen-year-old child!

At sixteen, I guess my early feminist impulses were already asserting themselves, because I did not understand these rules and found them intolerable.

I looked at her a long time, sitting at the far end of the cab, with her white-gloved hands neatly crossed, not saying a word. Finally she broke the silence with a peeved, "Well. . . ?" I thought, This is really unbelievable; she hasn't even moved an inch towards the door.

With that, I gave the cab driver *another* dollar, *another* quarter and *another* dime, "Take her back to where we came from," I said, and closed the door.

She was so bewildered and furious, she looked like a Natalie Wood doll that was about to explode.

For the rest of the evening I felt like Holden Caufield in *Catcher in the Rye*. I spent an hour outside the movie theater trying to sell her movie ticket, missed half of the movie, walked around Times Square and wound up on 42nd Street, where I played pinball machines in the arcades and acted very moody. I created a total atmosphere for myself.

That was not the version of the date I reported to my mother. She heard the "Archie and Veronica" version: we had a terrific time at the movies and had sodas afterwards, etc., etc., which of course she believed until my date's mother called the next day to ask my mother how I could treat her daughter that way.

Although my mother didn't admit that she approved of my behavior, she certainly roared with laughter when I told her the real story.

Steve James

Ninja master and actor Steve James has starred in the three *American Ninja* films. Other film credits include: *I'm Gonna Get You Sucka, To Live and Die in L.A., Hollywood Shuffle*, and *The Delta Force*. Steve is proficient in Tiger Claw Kung Fu, and other martial arts and street weapons.

When I was growing up in New York, my nickname was Lurch and my hero was Jim Brown. I was the biggest guy in the neighborhood, so I became "the protector," the fighter for the guys. It was kind of my release, because I was very, very shy around girls. I was particularly shy around Sharla, a hot number who I *knew* had been there. Oh, she was fine... Just gorgeous. Even though she had a beautiful figure and I wouldn't have minded exploring other parts of her body, I would have been happy *just* to kiss Sharla's lips.

Sharla went to another high school and would come to see our track meets. One day, before a 440 relay, I tried something out of an old Bill Cosby routine: I went into the locker room and I did, I don't know, quadruple push-ups, so that my muscles would be really pumped when I took off my sweats for the race. I went back out on the field, positioned myself in front of Sharla, and peeled off my sweats very slowly, looking out my peripheral vision, knowing she was what we called "tingling."

I won the race. That gave me enough guts, along with the pressure of the boys on the team waitin' to see if I was gonna score, to ask her for a date. While I was asking, I was praying she'd say no. When she accepted, I thought, Oh, god, this is my first date. What do I do?

I decided to take Sharla to a double bill. The second movie was *The Dirty Dozen*, which starred my idol, Jim Brown.

We were in back of the theater in the middle of the first show and nothing was happening. I tried to keep conversation going, crackin' the worst jokes, but I knew I was bombing. Then *The Dirty Dozen* started and Jim Brown suddenly became my inspiration.

Three quarters of the way into the film, I finally put my arm around her shoulders. Then, when Jim started tearing up the Nazis, I was able to bring her a little bit closer to me, but I was still scared to make that attempt to kiss. And I wanted to tongue-kiss her so bad. She had beautiful lips.

Finally, when Jim Brown got killed, I just totally grabbed her and kissed her passionately. Now Jim Brown was the last person to die in *The Dirty Dozen*, so this kiss started when the movie was pretty much over.

All of a sudden the lights came up. I was oblivious to what was goin' on. She said, "Stop, stop, Steven, stop, stop." I eventually looked up and of course these strangers that were sitting behind us were watching, like we were a third show. She said, "Well, let's go."

I couldn't. I was so excited I finally scored, it... um... showed in certain parts of my body. Real bad. I mean, I was standing up *very straight*, okay? If it was winter I wouldn't have minded, because I could hide it with a coat. But no, it was summer, you dig what I'm saying?

She started laughing. God bless her, it wasn't a cruel laugh. It was more of an embarrassed laugh for me. At the time I couldn't see it that way. I was so humiliated I couldn't finish the date or look at Sharla again. It was a total washout.

After what seemed like half an hour, I could safely get up from my seat. It probably wasn't that long, but I know the music at intermission was playing and everyone but the janitor had left the theater.

Next day the homeboys asked, "So how was it, man, with Sharla?"

"What'd you think, man? Shoot. They don't call me Lurch for nothin', shoot."

Of course, the truth came back to them through their girlfriends. But none of my homeboys came to me 'cause they probably figured I would have gotten real threatening with 'em and called up my inspiration, Jim Brown.

Waylon Jennings

BILLY MITCHELL

*Jessi Colter and husband
Waylon Jennings*

Grammy Award-winner Waylon Jennings has pushed country music forward from the Nashville Sound to the Outlaw movement, and broadened its audience, as evidenced by his thirteen gold albums. Waylon has collaborated with Willie Nelson, Johnny Cash, Kris Kristofferson as well as his wife, Jessi Colter.

Jessi was a late convert to country music. When she started, she liked the rock 'n' roll things, the pop things, and the gospel music, because her mother was a Pentecostal preacher. She's a great artist.

She had written a song that Duane Eddy, her husband at the time, had asked me to sing with her. It was a duet. We did a demo, and then I didn't see her again until 1968, after she and Duane were divorced.

She looked just as beautiful as the first time I met her: She had long, long black hair and was about eighteen inches around. She still is tiny; the waist is still the same.

We'd been around each other a little bit, and one day I asked her if she might like to go out.

I met her earlier that afternoon, we went out to dinner and then I went and worked that night at J.D.'s in Phoenix, Arizona. When I was finished, I said to her, "I'm hungry." I didn't wanna go to a restaurant so we went by the apartment.

I said, "You know how to fix scrambled egg sandwiches?" 'Cause that was my big deal at night. I loved them.

She said, "Yeah, I can make 'em."

I said, "Okay, make 'em."

She says, "Well, I'm gonna put a little mayonnaise on 'em," and I said, "I don't want no mayonnaise on 'em."

She says, "Well, get a little onion. Onions'll help 'em," and I said, "I don't want onions in 'em. I just want plain bread and plain scrambled eggs and salt and pepper."

"Naw," she said. "You need that. You don't know what's good."

She kept on 'til I said, "I'm gonna kill you if you don't fix my eggs like I want 'em." That's how bad it was!

She made me so mad. She did everything she could in every way to make me angry. She'd pick things out of me. I couldn't understand what it was: it just seemed like every time I turned around I was mad at her. Come to find out I wanted to get away from her so quick, but I didn't want to be rude and I was still hungry. That was the worst date I think I ever had, right there.

I didn't call her for awhile. Finally, I run into her about two weeks later and she says, "Why don't you call?" and I said, "You drive me crazy. What're you talking about? I never had anybody make me as mad as quick as you."

She says, "Well, that's my fault," and I said, "Well, I know it's your fault."

I said, "Why do you do that?" and she says, "I like to see the fire in you."

It must've been true love right off 'cause we got married one year later.

After all these years, the fire is still there. She's just found a new way of bringing it out of me.

Tom Jones

TREVOR LEIGHTON

Noted, since the sixties, for his openly sensuous performance style, Tom Jones attracted a new generation of fans when, in 1988, he successfully collaborated with the British avant-garde, techno-pop group The Art of Noise.

I was married when I was sixteen years old and had a son when I was seventeen years old. However, when I was eight years old, I got involved in a game of hopscotch with a twelve-year-old and vowed never to date an older woman again.

Lainie Kazan

Lainie Kazan has starred in dozens of theatrical plays and musicals, and has made numerous appearances on TV talk shows and series. Kazan has recorded five albums. Her film credits include: *One From the Heart*, *My Favorite Year* and *Lust in the Dust*.

It was a blind date with a major star who shall remain nameless. I was being detained by another major star, my hotshot hairdresser, Gene Shacove.

Gene had just cut and conditioned my hair, but I didn't have another hour to wait for him to finish drying it. So I dashed out of his salon with wet hair hoping to get home before my date.

The BMW was already parked in my driveway as I turned onto my street in Beverly Hills. Oh, no, I thought, I can't walk in and meet a big star for the first time looking like a bag lady who got caught under a lawn sprinkler! So I ran next door to my neighbor's and called my secretary.

"Can you get him to go out on the balcony in the back?"

"To do what?"

"Ask him if he needs to make a phone call."

He thought my secretary was crazy, but he went along with it. I snuck up through the front stairs and started to throw on clothes. I put on my electric blue corduroy minidress with the zipper that went all the way up the front and the big open brass rings on the sleeves, matching blue go-go boots, and lots of false eyelashes.

From the eyes down I looked great, but my hair was still a damp wreck, so I said to myself, it's 1969, the era of hairpieces, I'll stick on a fall.

This fall hung down to the bottom of my bra. I fastened it at the top with some pins and wrapped a print scarf around the joint.

I finally come down the stairs to meet this guy, who by now is quite nippy from having waited out on the balcony for me for almost one hour. He's charming and wonderful and more than ready to go to a party in the Valley.

We get into his BMW and I immediately notice this big, black, Great Dane filling up the back seat. That's fine. I don't mind dogs.

But this dog obviously missed dinner, because as soon as we start driving, the dog starts eating my hair. He's eating and eating. The hairpiece is shifting and moving. I'm shifting and I'm moving, trying to keep up with this voracious canine, but I'm hysterical. Simultaneously, I'm trying to be glamorous and entertaining because my date is a major movie star and I don't want to blow it.

Finally, just as the fall is about to fall off my head, I turn to this star and announce, "Excuse me, your dog is eating my hair. And my hair isn't mine."

He says without missing a beat, "Neither is mine," and whips off his toupee!

Well, I went into shock—literally went into shock! I mean, it was a brilliant comic move, but it took me several minutes before I could actually laugh. And once I did, we both couldn't stop.

Later, I realized what a courageous and generous man he was to go to such extremes to make me feel comfortable, but at the time, I truly thought he was nuts.

Obviously that didn't faze him, because at the next gas station he replaced his piece, I replaced mine, and we both went off to the party.

Stepfanie Kramer

Stepfanie Kramer portrays the tough-minded detective, Dee Dee McCall, in the crime show, *Hunter*. Her diverse television credits include the mini-series *Favorite Son* and the TV movie *Take My Daughters, Please*.

My boyfriend in high school came by to take me out for ice cream just after sunset one spring evening. This was one of our favorite things to do.

I get into his $200 clunker and we start to drive over to the Baskin Robbins. After a few minutes, I notice that we aren't taking the normal route. I'm thinking, Maybe we're going to a different Baskin Robbins that's farther out. We lived in the San Fernando Valley, which at the time was an area with a lot of open fields and horse ranches. Or maybe we're just taking a nicer drive? We're alone together, it's romantic. What the hell?

As we pull onto a rather dark, little, country road, all of a sudden police lights come on behind us and I see it's one of those unmarked cars with an interior light that sits on the back panel, not the dash.

My boyfriend starts to pull over and becomes very upset.

I say, "What's the matter? You weren't speeding or anything?"

He says, "The cops are pulling us over, that's why I'm upset," in a tone that's really irritable.

"What's wrong? Why are you upset?" I'm really quite confused.

"I have fifteen outstanding tickets," he snaps back. "I'm sure they've gone to warrant."

I don't say anything, but I'm thinking, Boy, are you stupid; how did this happen?

Within seconds, two plainclothes policemen get out of their car and come up along both sides of our car. They shine their flashlights inside and show us their ID. With each of their gestures, my date is becoming more and more agitated.

They look at his driver's license. "Is this your correct address?"

"Yes."

Then they run through some other very specific information which makes it clear that they've run down his plates.

One of the cops says, "Would you step out of the car, please? You have fifteen outstanding warrants."

Oh, god, he's right!

My boyfriend starts to get out of the car and I can see he's absolutely on the edge of this panicked energy. They turn him around, they put his hands on the roof, they start to pat him down, and he suddenly shouts, "Don't touch me, man. Don't pat me down," Inside I'm saying, "Hey, relax! Shhh, it's all right."

He's shouting, "Don't, man Don't do that. Don't you—" Then he loses it. He whips around, grabs one cop's gun and points it first at him, then at the other cop on my side of the car, screaming at the top of his lungs, "Don't you touch me! Don't you touch me!!"

Then he hisses, "I'm gonna kill ya."

I'm thinking, Oh, my god. I just wanted an ice cream cone! Outside he's screaming bloody murder, "Goddamnit, get the hell... Put your hands over your head, man! Over your goddamn head!"

He marches these cops back to their car. Both of their car doors are open. He forces them to lay down in the front seat and he fires twice, *right at them*! Then he takes the gun, throws it off into a field, and comes running back to me.

By this time, I've slid across the seat and out the driver's side of the car. I'm standing there muttering, "I'm in *The Twilight Zone*.

This *must* be *The Twilight Zone*," when he grabs me and starts shaking me and cries, "We gotta get outta here. I shot 'em. I shot 'em. We gotta get outta here!"

I'm saying, "No, no, *we* don't gotta do anything." Trying to calm him down.

He pleads, "No, no. No, we gotta go, we...Are you with me? Are you with me?"

"With you?"

"With me, with me! What day is this? What day is this? What day is this?" He's yelling and he's shaking me.

I'm scared to death, but I say,. "I don't know...it's...... it's, it's Tuesday, it's Tuesday."

He screams, "No, *what day is it*?"

"I don't know...Um, um...April. April first."

"*April first? April first?*" Then he shouts, "APRIL FOOL!!!" And starts laughing hysterically.

Two seconds later, he whistles back towards the police car and hollers, "Hey guys!" And the two "dead policemen" get up and shout, "Oh, boy, we really pulled one on her. She really bought it, didn't she?" Slapping each other and going on and on.

I burst into tears. I was sixteen and utterly horrified.

Then my boyfriend says, "I guess she didn't think it was that funny."

What was funny, however, was what happened to him about a year and a half later. He went to jail. Not for outstanding parking warrants, but for something else. And after that, he became a producer. If this episode is any indication of his ability to make a convincing, visual sell, I'm sure he's doing quite well.

Sherry Lansing

FRED OHRINGER

In January 1980, Sherry Lansing became president of 20th Century-Fox Productions, making her the first woman to hold that position. Lansing and her partner Stanley Jaffe have jointly produced *Black Rain*, *The Accused*, *Fatal Attraction*, *Firstborn*, *Racing With the Moon*, and two movies for television.

I am a huge basketball fan.

For years I used to go to all the Laker games. I had seats that were terrific and I admired all the players. Among all those athletes, there obviously are several players that you get crushes on, but there was one player in particular I thought was adorable.

Fade in twenty years later. I'm at a big party at some friends' house, and this adorable player is among the group of fifty people. I happen to be there alone. So was he.

We started talking and he was absolutely delightful and absolutely charming. We just hit it off. As I left the party, he asked where he could reach me, and sure enough he called me at the office the next day. I called him back at his office and we set up a time for dinner.

My secretary, who's a huge basketball fan and knew what an incredible player he had been, was thrilled for me. "Just think," she said, "You used to sit and watch this guy twenty years ago and now you have a date with him, God, isn't this exciting?"

It was more than exciting; it was a childhood dream come true. I'd always wanted to go out with a basketball star ever since I dated a college All-America basketball player when I was the captain of the high school cheerleading squad. Thinking about the fantasy made me feel like an adolescent anticipating a first date.

The day of the date was so crazy, I skipped lunch so that I could go home early from the office and get ready. I washed my hair and I thought real hard about what I was going to wear and I put on makeup and I really thought I looked as good as I could.

He was charming and lovely when he came to pick me up at my house in Beverly Hills at seven. We got into the car and he started driving and driving. I said, "Where are you going?" He said, "There's this great new restaurant in Pasadena." Pasadena is an hour away from my house.

I thought, This is so peculiar, but who am I to say anything?

As we drove, he asked me about making movies. I asked him about life after basketball. He was doing something every bit as attractive but unrelated to sports.

We get to this restaurant and my instinct said something's wrong. Why would someone drive an hour to come to this average place? Once again, I didn't say anything.

The table wasn't quite ready when we walked in, so we sat down in the waiting area and ordered appetizers and drinks. I then said to him, "Well, tell me a little bit more about your personal life while we wait. Have you ever been married?"

He said "Yes."

I said. "Do you have any children?"

He said, "Two."

I said, "Well, how long has it been since you've been divorced?"

He said, "I'm not divorced."

I said, "Well, how long has it been since you've been separated?"

He said, "I'm not exactly separated..."

I remember thinking, I'm starving. I can't believe I'm hearing this story before the appetizers.

"How could you have done this?" I demanded.

"Well, I was real attracted to you...and, and...I knew that if I told you the truth that you wouldn't go because I know what kind of person you are, and I'm not happily married and I just, you know, ah..."

"Look, I don't care what your problem is. You were at the party alone; I had no way of knowing you were married. Now I understand why we drove all the way to Pasadena! Just take me home."

"Can't, can't we—just, just get a salad?"

"I don't want anything to eat, I'd rather have a tunafish sandwich at home!"

Then we got up and left. I mean the place must have thought we were nuts.

I didn't say a word to him the whole one-hour ride home. Although I sure felt like saying, I'm not passing judgment on anybody else's life-style, but I do know what my own moral code is : I don't go out with married men. And I resent the fact that, by withholding information, you took my choice away.

As soon as I got in the door, I called my secretary. She said, "It's nine o'clock. What're you doing home already? What did he do?" I said, "Put it this way, character and talent are two very different things." I just thought it was the worst thing anyone could ever do to a single person.

At the same time, I was laughing, thinking, I have clean hair, I have makeup on, I'm wearing a pretty outfit, it's nine o'clock: who can I call up and ask to take me out?

Barbara Lazaroff

CHIP STONE

Barbara Lazaroff,
husband Wolfgang Puck
and lobster

Partner of renowned chef Wolfgang Puck, designer/co-owner of Spago, Spago Toyko and Chinois on Main, Barbara Lazaroff is an architectural interior designer especially well known for her innovative restaurant concepts.

I never wanted to get married. Never wanted to *be* married. But I said, Look, if this Jewish broad from the Bronx is going to get married, I'm going to do it like a princess. Because certainly, with regard to married life, you only get to be a princess once... unless you marry a prince! So I decided to plan a wedding that should be on "The Rich and Shameless," as I refer to it.

We were married in a fifteenth century village in the south of France in a fairy tale sort of wedding that I spent a year planning. I had horse-drawn carriages and knights in shining armor, medieval trumpeters and jugglers. The festivities lasted seventeen hours. It was really filmed for *Lifestyles of the Rich and Famous.*

So here was this "supposedly" glorious, romantic, wedding. It's going to work out. Right? Right. Supposedly...

We had, on our honeymoon, his parents and my parents. His parents are from a little town in the countryside of Austria. They don't speak English, and are rather sheltered in terms of their experiences. I don't speak German. My parents are urban, but they haven't traveled a lot either. In spite of this, we all seemed to get along quite well.

We were staying at Le Crillon, one of the most elegant hotels in the world. The first night, we all go out to dinner. Thank God, it wasn't La Tour d'Argent! It was more of a casually chic type restaurant. Almost Spago-style for Paris. Very popular at the time, but certainly not black-tie.

Unfortunately, I ordered one of my favorite foods, lobster.

Now, Wolf's father is a highly adventurous man, except for his palate, which is definitely narrow. In fact, he has a major aversion to all sorts of food. He wanted his son to be a carpenter, and he told his son, often, that cooking was sissy work.

So, I'm eating this lobster and his father starts making the most awful noises at the table, and begins sticking his finger down his throat and going "Gag, gag," . . . trying to explain to me with metacommunications (knowing I do not understand German), that lobster makes him want to throw up.

I turn to Wolf and say quietly, "Wolf, please. Tell your father to stop doing that at the table. Okay?"

Wolf doesn't answer me. His father continues to feign gagging. My mother pretends not to notice and I'm losing my appetite.

"Please, Wolf," I say now through clenched teeth.

"Look, I'm not going to tell my father. You tell him."

"He doesn't understand what I'm talking about!"

And we proceeded, on our honeymoon, to get into the worst fight at the table. It got completely out of hand, with everybody yelling.

Wolf huffs out of the restaurant, his parents in tow. We all go back to the Crillon, in separate taxis. And we all stomp off in different directions. Wolf's father's not speaking to me. My parents aren't speaking to his parents. His mother's not speaking to his father. Wolf's not speaking to me. To top it off, Wolf decides that he's leaving. He's going back to America tomorrow. Forget it! It's a nightmare!

The next morning, Wolf took his parents to the Palais de

Versailles, and my parents and I commiserated in their room. I didn't know what the hell to do!

Distraught, I go down to the concierge and I tell him I need somebody to translate this eight-page letter that I wrote, from English into German. He sends me off to the Language Institute, which is in a really ritzy area, Faubourg St. Honoré, where all the couture houses are. Truthfully, I was tempted to buy out the *entire* neighborhood with *his* credit card. Instead, I tell the translator I'm desperate. She tells me she can give me the letter in two days. I tell her it's my honeymoon. She tells me to pick it up three hours later. The French understand *l'amour*.

I bring the translation to their room, and there was all this crying and...making up. Wolf's father finally understood that I wasn't angry at him, I was angry at Wolf. And when he understood that, he said to his son, "I don't care if she's angry at you. That's *your* problem." But, of course, I really wasn't angry at anyone, at least not anymore. And we decided to stay married...which has been great. Because I discovered I did marry a prince...on some days anyway. So sometimes I get to be a princess after all.

Timothy Leary

SMEAL/GALELLA, LTD.

Timothy and Barbara Leary

A former professor and drug researcher, Timothy Leary is a psychologist, author, stand-up philosopher, computer exponent, designer of reactive videoware for Mental Fitness, screenwriter and actor. He is currently president of Futique, a producer of electronic books and other interactive media.

Bad dates. That's so negative. I'm into positive thinking. So I'll tell you a good date.

I'm certainly monogamous. I'd have to go back forty years and even then you'd meet someone and decide you're not going to meet them again. That's it.

On my first date with my current wife, Barbara, we had lunch, and after lunch I drove her home. Then I went back to my place, picked up a book I had written called *What Does Woman Want?* and dropped it off at her house. She liked the book so much, she stayed up all night reading it. In the morning, she phoned and told me what she wanted... Marriage.

And we've been married ever since. That's a good date.

It's the only time I gave anyone that book. I don't know what would happen if I ever tried it again.

Jerry Lee Lewis

JUDY WILLIAMS

Perhaps best known for the songs "Whole Lotta Shakin' Goin' On" and "Great Balls of Fire," singer Jerry Lee was inducted into the Rock and Roll Hall of Fame in 1986. Since 1981, he has expanded his repertoire and recordings to include country music.

Jerry Lee Lewis, his wife, Kerrie, and their son

The first time I asked out my wife, Kerrie, in August 1983, it got so turned around I didn't think she would ever see me again.

I was receiving the Elvis Presley Distinguished Achievement Award this special evening from Memphis State University and I asked Kerrie to go. I'd known Kerrie since she was ten years old when she recorded my song "Whole Lotta Shakin'." After that, she and her two sisters, who also sing, opened quite a few of my shows.

I was very excited about my first date with twenty-year-old Kerrie since I had been wanting to go out with her for several weeks. I told her to meet me at the September Place Nightclub because I did not know how to get to her house. When I arrived forty-five minutes later (I had overslept and got a late start), Kerrie was gone.

Well, I waited for thirty minutes at the nightclub; she never showed up. I headed towards the Holiday Inn Rivermont, where the above event was being held, and Kerrie was there waiting for me, looking beautiful in a white silk dress. Needless to say, she was upset, but she didn't show it. I had a real hard time explaining that I did go to our meeting place and waited for her. She admitted that she didn't think I stood her up, but knowing me as well as she did for ten years, she really didn't know what to think about me being late. I told her to think the truth, that I was late because I overslept. She just laughed and said, "I should have known."

To make it up to Kerrie, we danced all night, and needless to say, I have never been late again, maybe a little early... And to this day, when it comes to just "us," I am "on time...."

David Lynch

David Lynch's films include *Eraserhead*, *Dune*, *The Elephant Man* and *Blue Velvet*. For television he conceived and directed the pilot for the TV series, *Twin Peaks*.

KIMBERLY WRIGHT

When I was in the first grade, I had a girlfriend, and I went home for lunch every day. One lunchtime, before going home, I walked my girlfriend to her house and told her I would pick her up after lunch and we would walk back to school together. She said she'd be there.

After lunch, I went to her house and rang the doorbell. But no one answered. I rang the doorbell again. And no one answered. I rang the doorbell again. And no one answered. I rang the doorbell until about three o'clock that afternoon because I was *positive* she was in there.

But then I had to go back to school.

I got to school just about the time it was over for the day. And there she was... in the class, not in her house.

I couldn't believe it. How could she possibly be in two places at once? It was almost like a magical act.

Virginia Madsen

 Actress Virginia Madsen's credits for film, TV and cable include: *Dune, Modern Girls, Slamdance, The Hitchhiker, Mr. North, Moonlighting, Gotham, Heart of Dixie* and *Third Degree Burn.*

I never had a date in high school. I was always everybody's friend.

I assumed it was because most of the guys were embarrassed to be seen with me. I wasn't pretty in the preppy pretty way. I had strange curly hair and I dressed weirdly. You might say, I was sort of a peculiar, hippie child in the seventies, which was a very odd combination.

If I were content with being odd, things might have been okay. But, unfortunately, I was also one of those people who was always trying to be in the popular crowd. I'd get invited to the popular crowd's parties at somebody's mansion, but when I got there, I'd overhear people saying loudly, and for my benefit, "What's she doing here?"

It was at these parties that I had the closest thing to a series of identical bad dates.

There was always that one guy who all the girls wanted and who had that four-year girlfriend. Something would be going on between them—they'd be breaking up or fighting, who knows—and suddenly I'd realize that young man in distress had his eye on me.

I would immediately become self-conscious and think, Oh, my God, he's looking at me. He probably thinks I'm weird. Then, to my amazement, he would come over and start talking to me. Very quickly he'd ask if I'd go up to the second floor with him to the "make-out" rooms.

I was always hesitant. "I really don't know...I..."

"No, no, no, come on," he'd assure me. "I just wanna talk to you."

We'd go up to the bedrooms, and it would be really romantic. I'd think, Oh gosh, things are going to change from here on. Then he'd kiss me, and I'd be thinking, Wow, I'm kissing a boy, isn't this wonderful? After that, without fail, he'd start to cry.

It was the most bizarre thing. It was always the same sequence: First there had to be the kiss, then the crying, then the confession of all his problems—the troubles with the girlfriend, the pressures of high school, how tough it was to be popular. I would sympathize and the guy would always respond, "I didn't know you were like this. You're so great and so easy to talk to. I can't believe I feel so much better."

I'd nod and listen, like a psychiatrist, and then he'd pull back from me with fear. "You won't tell anybody any of the things I said, will you?" I'd assure him that I'd keep his secrets, which I did, and then we'd return to the party together and immediately go off in different directions. If I came over to say even "hi," the guy would cower with embarrassment.

Five minutes later, he'd tell his buddies how he'd screwed me. As a result, I had quite a reputation for a virgin.

John Matuszak

Six-foot eight-inch John Matuszak was an All-Pro football player for the Raiders, an NFL number-one draft choice, an actor (*North Dallas Forty, Ice Pirates, Caveman*) and author of *Cruisin' with the Tooz*, an account of his wild days on and off the field.

I just think chicks are great! Six out of ten of my favorite people in the world are women: my mother, my three sisters, my niece, that's five, and my lady, that's, six. It's always been like that. And women have always liked me.

Some women are into the image. Some aren't. Usually the best times are with the ones who don't know who you are, but, like Hugh Hefner said, "That's fine. Let 'em be into the image. Whatever it is, as long as I get some."

When I was with the Raiders, one time, Kenny Stabler and I, we were both up in Tahoe and we had adjoining suites. It was real interesting. We kept our doors open and the girls were just streamin' in and out. Back then it was a lot different. Then, the worst thing that would happen to you, you could get a shot for it. Nowadays I'm a lot more cautious.

A couple of years ago I was at some party for the opening of a tailor shop in Beverly Hills and I saw this beautiful oriental girl. She had this gorgeous, black dress. The sleeves, they were all

149

black feathers. The rest of the dress was leather mixed with lace.
Leather and lace, with feathers...over a great body...*And* hair
down to her butt, watch out!!

I walked up to her and said I'd like to have lunch some time. I
guess she knew who I was and gave me her number. We called a
few times and had dinner a couple of times. Then one night, when
I had just planned another nice dinner, she drove up to my house
in her Mercedes (she was independently wealthy, I guess),
knocked on my door, and when I opened it she said, "Would you
like me to spend the night?"

I said, "What about dinner?" I wasn't prepared for this at all.

"We can eat here...," she smiled and walked right in with her
overnight bag.

It was all packed. This girl was prepared!

We had this fantastic night together. She was madly in love with
me. I think I was in love with her, but it might have been lust. Or a
little of both.

When she got up the next morning, she was like a different
person. She just hid her face and ran into the bathroom. I thought
that was awfully odd. But I couldn't read the expression on her face
because when you've got hair down that long, all you gotta do is
just turn your head a little bit and it covers pretty good.

That was it. She just didn't return my calls anymore. I tried her,
but after three or four calls, I realized that this girl wasn't "woman
enough" to call back and say, "Look, I've got something else going
on. Just back off." Because she was definitely single. No rings on
her fingers and no neckties in her closet.

When she finally did call, she said, "I didn't call because I was
too much in love with you." That's what I call a pretty bad date.

Minnesota Fats

World's Greatest Pool Player, World's Greatest Card Player, World's Greatest TV Host, World's Greatest Talker— he's Minnesota Fats.

Bad dates? I never had a bad date in my life. I always had a lot of women. I went out with Mae West, Texas Carmine, Helen Morgan, Ginger Lynn. All the stars were friends of mine. Jane Russell, Judy Garland, Zsa Zsa Gabor's a good friend of mine. You know, I had a show, *Celebrity Billiards*, did you know that? And every star in Hollywood—George Burns, Milton Berle, Nanette Fabray, Phyllis Diller—all of them were on that show. But I don't know how I feel about a bad date.

I never had any problems at all. I learned everything I know from other people's problems. I got to be a genius. You know I'm the world's greatest talker, did you know that? Well, I am. Because I won the championship of the world twice in Canada alone. I can talk from now to the year 2000 and never repeat myself. But as far as bad dates, I had *more women* than anybody on earth. And I don't know why I still have.

You know you can't get any older than me, did you know that? They got me eighty-three to one-hundred in the world. No living creature on the earth knows *how old* I am. But they all know *who* I am. There's no place on earth I'm not known. But when it comes to women...

I have no idea if I'm great or what it is. It's next to ridiculous! I go dancing every night here in Nashville at the Stockyards Inn. Six nights a week, they're not open on Sunday. There's eighty-six bar stools in The Stockyards, and the most gorgeous... You know, Tennessee is famous for gorgeous creatures, you know that, don't you? The most gorgeous. They'll sit on them bar stools, nightly— thirty or forty girls, eight, nine, ten o'clock at night, waiting, with their tongues hanging out, to dance with me alone.

Most are in their early thirties, you know, not over thirty-five or forty. That don't mean nothin', age, anyhow. Ya see, a woman could be gorgeous beyond compare, fifty, sixty years old, if she happened to be that lucky. Could be Miss America tonight! All the care and treatment in the world ain't gonna help you. You just gotta *be* that way, you know what I mean?

But I never have to worry about women. They stand in line... just to dance with me. I dance pretty good. Not like them drunks, you know, up and down, kickin' high. I dance the Texas Two Step they holler about here. I don't make no big show out of it or nothing.

When I was two years old, I was sitting on the pool table. You see, I hung in saloons from mornin' till night, never drank in my life. Never smoke or drank. Just played pool. See people think pool is round balls in a green table. In every country it's a different situation. I play every facet. But I conquered all that before I was fifteen years old.

Did you know I can beat anybody living on earth playing any kind of cards? I'm known the world over for gambling. I'm a noted authority. Whenever there's an argument in Monaco or Vegas... That's how I met Fatima.

Fatima danced for me in Istanbul in the Sultan's Palace. She danced for me in Iran in the Shah's father's palace. She danced for me in the Casino Egypt at the Shepherd Hotel. I went with her. Then her daughter tried to nail me forty years later in Vegas. I was very busy at the time with something else, so I didn't wind up with her. It's unbelievable, but it's the way it is.

So like I say, I never had bad dates and I don't have 'em today. Hey, there's people, real good lookin' men, forty-five, fifty, you know what I mean, handsome lookin' guys, they watch me with the girls and they say, "Boy, you just amaze me every time I see you." I says, "Well, I can't help it." Because beautiful women...I was always crazy about beautiful women. And they was always chasing me around. Even at my age. I don't know how to even explain it.

And there's no way you can give lessons. I tell them all the time. You know, some smart crackers, once in a while, they say, "Oh, I don't know Fats..." I say, "Let me tell you a secret, young man. When *I* was *your age*, they chased me around with *mattresses* on their backs!"

People, I don't want to mention their names because they're in the limelight, too, but you wouldn't believe what they do. Followed me two-thousand miles. Heard I was here. Heard I was there. Do anything. A lot of stars. Not stars. Even midgets.

I used to have midgets, in the olden days, back when Broadway was my beat. I used to play in big theaters, backstage circuses, and stuff like that. And these little midgets on the bill, they was crazy about me. But they was just too tiny. We used to have a lot of fun. 'Cause I never had no hangups like other people.

Maybe that's why I never had no bad dates. I mean, every human can have bad dates, that's nothing to have. As a whole, they should have bad dates. But the good ones make up for that, you understand. That's the secret to all that.

Andre Miripolsky

Artist Andre Miripolsky produces sculptures, paintings, light-board drawings, clothing, jewelry, tapestries and album covers.

My personal life is pretty drab. That's not where I put my energy, it seems. I paint. But when a friend suggested a blind date with a woman designer, I said, Okay, I need a change.

"I've been on blind dates before," I told the date. "Usually my mother fixed me up. It was a drag." She agreed and said she wanted to come up with something interesting and memorable. Something that would keep the notion of blindness and just deal with personalities, like a telephone.

She came up with this idea of wearing paper bags over our heads. I went for it right away. I thought it was really cute.

I got a paper bag, cut out the holes and everything—eyes, nose and mouth—put it over my head, and went to her house. There was a note on the door saying, "Come in." I entered, looked around through the eye holes. There was beer on the coffee table and another note that said, "Wait here." She was taking a shower or something.

It was pretty wild just coming in there like that. We did have mutual friends, but I guess there was some kind of trust or something. And it made the expectation better. Actually, kind of kinky.

So I sat there with the bag over my head checking out the place, trying to figure out what she was like by the little clues and hints.

The way she lived. The objects she collected. The things she threw away. This went on for about ten minutes until she came out.

I thought, "The body's fine. The body without the head. Then she sat down and started talking.

We chatted with the bags over heads for about ten or fifteen minutes. Finally, I couldn't deal with the suspense anymore and took the bag off my head. She took hers off too.

She was a girl I'd avoided all through high school.

I wanted to put the bag right back on my head and slip out the door, but I found myself spending the next two hours comparing notes on the kids from our high school.

Thomas S. Monaghan

Thomas Monaghan is founder and chairman of the board of Domino's Pizza, Inc., and owner of the Detroit Tigers Baseball Club.

I'm the first to admit being a Frank Lloyd Wright fanatic. Ever since childhood, I've admired and respected Mr. Wright's work. And I've never passed up a chance to visit one of the great architect's magnificent structures... even if it meant snubbing a date.

One evening in particular, I remember picking up my date and, during the course of conversation, learning her parents lived in a home designed by Mr. Wright.

Immediately, I pulled the car over, turned it around and proceeded in the direction of her parents' home. Unfortunately, I completely forgot about my date. All that was on my mind was a chance to see the inside of her parents' house.

I spent the rest of the evening talking to her father about the house and his experiences working with Mr. Wright.

For obvious reasons, the date and romance never worked out. But that didn't stop me from having a most enjoyable evening... a point I'm sure my date wouldn't agree with me on.

Chris Monger

SUZANNE HANOVER

Born in Wales, Chris Monger came to America to show the films he made for Britain's Channel 4 at the Museum of Modern Art in New York and Filmex in L.A., and decided to stay. He wrote and directed *Waiting for the Light*, starring Shirley MacLaine and Teri Garr.

I'd fancied her for a long time but didn't even know her name. One day I bumped into her with a mutual friend and got to talk: we were both planning to see a band late that night at a sleazy club in the red light district. Seizing my chance, and using the fact that the Yorkshire Ripper was prowling such neighborhoods, I offered to pick her up and take her. She refused, saying she'd meet me there: she'd wait in the foyer. She was keeping her distance—but it was a date of sorts.

Before I left my apartment, I was gripped with insecurity and quickly changed my clothes two or three times. I was determined to make a good impression. I ended up wearing my original selection, and was now already running late.

As I roared down the street, a cat ran out from a dark alley. I didn't have a chance of stopping; as soon as I saw it, I heard the sickening crunch under my back wheels. I pulled over and looked in the rearview mirror. To my horror, the cat was still alive, writhing in mutilated agony.

I got out and walked towards it, knowing that I'd have to put it out of its misery. I'm not exactly macho-man and the very thought made me nauseous.

I reached the cat in time to see it give a last convulsive heave, and die. I stared at the poor creature with mixed emotions. I was saddened yet relieved. Out of the darkness a voice said:

"That's old Mrs. Jones's cat. Don't worry. I'll come with you."

I turned to find a middle-aged man staring at me, and the cat.

So now I'm walking down a dark lane, carrying a very squashed cat to tell an aged widow that I've killed her only companion. Great.

The house was in darkness. He knocked loudly and my mind raced trying to find the appropriate apology. There was silence within. He knocked again while I prayed that she was deaf, or at least asleep. My prayers were answered, again there was no reply.

"Leave it under the garden hedge. I'll see her in the morning." I didn't suggest we knock again, but left the cat, thanked the man(!), and raced back to the car. Now I was very late, with a highly ludicrous excuse.

When I pulled up outside the club, I was encouraged to see that she was still waiting just inside the doors. She was wearing a white minidress. She looked absolutely stunning. However, she also looked pretty pissed off.

I rushed in, pulling my most apologetic expression, and gave her a friendly peck on the cheek. I drew back and heard her scream. And scream.

I'd put two bloody handprints on her skirt. I didn't have a chance to say anything. She just ran to the ladies' room and never spoke to me again. I was late, I'd ruined her skirt, and I was obviously the Yorkshire Ripper.

Her best friend came out of the ladies room and listened to my story. She thought it was hilarious and bought me a drink to calm me down. We went home together that night and were together for several months.

But it's still my worst, and shortest, date, ever.

David Burton Morris and
Victoria Wozniak

David Burton Morris and Victoroia Wozniak with their kids

David Burton Morris is a director. For film, he directed *Loose Ends, Purple Haze, Patti Rocks, Hometown Boy Makes Good*; for TV, *Vietnam War Story, Tales from the Crypt* and *China Beach*. He is married to Victoria Wozniak.

Victoria Wozniak's feature-film writing credits include: *Loose Ends, Purple Haze, Heartbreak Hotel, Class Action, The Contender, Gangster of Love* and *Hidden Agenda*.

It was the spring of 1970 and I was driving back from campus in Minneapolis (they'd just burned down the ROTC!) and I saw this little girl hippie on the side of the road with bell-bottom jeans and no shoes.

I was carrying my shoes.

Dirty feet. She probably didn't shave under her arms either, but I couldn't check.

That's not true, David, I always shaved under my arms.

She had really long curly hair and looked kind of cute so I swung over and picked her up. I asked her where she was going, and it turned out that she lived with her parents three blocks away

159

from my parents' house. I couldn't believe that I'd never seen her before.

I remembered later that I'd heard of him. He was part of a rich kid's gang in Highland Village, and someone as a joke had once told them there was a party at my parents' house. All these guys showed up and my mother told them there was no party, but a couple of them hung around at the back door anyway. I was in eighth grade at the time, so my sister and I made them popcorn and giggled. Then one of the guys started throwing around our kitty. I remember that a David Morris stopped this guy from hurting a cat. That's the only time I ever remember hearing his name.

I was a hero.

He was. But in 1970 he looked to me like a bourgeois hippie. He had a white Camaro and a ponytail all the way down his back...

I still do.

And nice *creases* down the middle of his bell-bottom jeans. That's what *really* tipped me off. I was very heavily into political things and he had all this jewelry on, lots of rings and this expensive photographic equipment in the back of his car.

So we got to my parents' house by the river and I asked him if he wanted to get high. He said sure. I went into the house and I got this killer dope that some vets had given me and brought it out. In those days, you didn't just take one or two hits, you smoked the whole joint, and with this stuff, one hit and you were dead. Which I didn't tell David.

I took one hit and passed the joint to David. We took a walk by the river and he smoked the whole thing. I knew how incredibly screwed up he had to be, but he continued to act cool. He said, "Well, do you want me to come back or call you?" I said, "Whatever you want." I didn't care, I *swear* I never expected to see him again. He left.

Forty-five minutes later, he was back at my door. "Vicki, what did you do to me? I can't do anything!" Then he came down and sat around with me and played guitar in my basement. Nothing else happened.

Several months later, during the summer, we ended up spending the night at this house he was sharing with a bunch of people down by the St. Croix River, and it was a disaster.

The worst in my life.

David!

Vicki was a virgin.

I was not!

She acted like it.

Pretty close, though.

Everything she knew, she'd read about in a book, and it wasn't very exciting.

He was used to women who were a lot more experienced than I was.

She sat there like this stiff, and that's not the part that's supposed to be stiff.

David!

After it was all over with, I said, "Well, that wasn't too great, was it?" She agreed. I said, "Listen, let's not pursue this sex aspect 'cause if we just keep doing this I'll probably dump you and move on rather quickly. Let's just remain friends."

So we did. He and I became best friends. We even slept in the same bed, but not with each other. (No one knew that!)

Then, three years later, Vicki raped me.

Not exactly!

And we've been together for seventeen years.

That's true.

You know, I never really thought about this incident in terms of second chances. I just think about what would have happened if I had kept on driving by on that road—just seeing her figure getting smaller in my rearview mirror. The decision to make love again or to carry on a relationship wasn't a big decision (she was my best friend). The decision was breaking for the first time. If I had just sneezed or dropped a cigarette, I would have missed her. If I had, it would have made all the difference to the last twenty years of my life.

Mark Mothersbaugh

Mark Mothersbaugh is co-founder of the conceptual art rock band DEVO, a composer and an artist.

Nancye Ferguson and Mark Mothersbaugh

Worst dates are very subjective. For instance, some people might think the first date I had with my girlfriend Nancye Ferguson was a pretty bad date. Nancye and I thought it was inspired.

It was Halloween night and Nancye and her band of three little girls (six, eight, and ten years old), all four of whom wore holy communion dresses, were playing at a local club. I didn't know Nancye well at the time, but I was attracted to her and was looking for an excuse to ask her out. I thought I might get that chance after her set.

While I was watching the four communion girls sing, a beautiful woman came up to me and said, "Do you really know how to use a whip like you do in your video, 'Whip It'?"

I said, "No. That was just a video trick."

"Well, would you like to come home and see me whip the clothes off my sister?"

I said, "That could be interesting."

After Nancye's band stopped playing, I said to her, "Do you want to go see somebody whip the clothes off her sister?"

She said, "That could be interesting."

We could have followed the whipping sisters in my car, but we got talked into, "It's too difficult to find the place..." Har, har, har.

The house had several levels and was built into a hill. It looked pretty normal—except for lots of parrots and boa constrictors.

They showed us their collection of boa constrictors and then they said, "We also have tattoos!" Now, if you've got body tattoos, you don't want to just look at them in the mirror by yourself. So they did a "clinical strip" for us, talking about each tattoo as they slowly exposed. They had a whole presentation. It was their esthetic. It was art. They were human art pieces.

One sister had a body covered in tiger tattoos. Then this guy came in. He didn't have anything to say. He just was there so that he could show off his zebra stripes that went from his neck to his knee pits.

Then the whip artist took off her clothes and she had a boa constrictor tattoo that started at her knees and wrapped around her leg three times, with the boa's head ready to strike her private parts. She had shaved the hair in the shape of a heart and dyed it bright red to match the hair on top of her head. They all had nipple rings and lip rings to accent the look.

I thought all this was pretty interesting, but Nancye was probably thinking, I just met this guy. Do you think he knew any of this was going to happen before we got here?

Meanwhile, the whipper proceeded to get drunk. So drunk, she jumped on top of me and tried to get me in bed. After that didn't work, she jumped on Nancye and tried and tried to get her into bed.

I thought about leaving, but we didn't have a car.

Somewhere during this thing of showing us the boa constrictors, jumping us, and marching us up to her bedroom (which was covered with DEVO records), the whipper started to perform a fashion show of leather gear and other exotic paraphenalia she pulled out of her stuffed closet. The look was somewhere between "Warlock" and "Deep Purple." She talked through the whole thing, half-incoherently, and finally ended up wearing nothing but a purple, velvet cape. None of this, however, got us to take our clothes off.

Nancye wasn't saying much through all of this. She couldn't

believe what was going on. And the whipper couldn't believe that
we weren't responding properly.

"You're too uptight," she complained. "I can't believe you're not
into making love." I explained once again to her that this was the
first time Nancye and I had been out together and Nancye wasn't
in the mood to make love with them. (I can understand that.)

Fed up with me, the whipper got even more plastered and
announced it was time for her whip act. She and her sister walked
out a bedroom window and stepped onto the roof. We followed.
But as the whipper put her hand over her head to fling the whip at
her clothed sister, she suddenly lost her balance and fell backwards
off the roof.

For a second we wondered if this was part of the act. In fact, we
were still wondering what was going on when her sister ran over,
and then we all ran over to the edge of the roof and looked down.

There she was...lying there on her back. We were sure that she
must have broken her neck and died.

The next thing I remember is Nancye and I calling 911, trying to
get the paramedics to this house. Good thing the whipper was
drunk, because the fall just knocked the air out of her. By the time
the paramedics got there, she was up stamping around in nothing
but her purple cape cursing, "Oh, shit! Oh, shit!"

About five in the morning, after the paramedics finally left, the
tiger-tattooed sister drove us back to my car. Then I drove Nancye
home at sunrise. We exchanged phone numbers and decided to go
out some time. Because we didn't do much talking that night—
except for how to try and get a paramedic.

The evening gave us such high expectations for the rest of our
relationship, that on our second date, we stayed home. We sat in
front of the TV, and well...avoided whips.

But don't think the whip artist was forgotten! We were duly
impressed by these people. She was an inspiration!

Years later I ran into her and she told me, "Oh, by the way,
Mark, I joined the circus."

"That's interesting. Do you use your whip?"

Shirley Muldowney

Shirley Muldowney broke the gender barrier in drag racing. Three-time winner of the Winston Championships, Muldowney had her career documented in the feature film, *Heart Like a Wheel*.

JEFF KATZ

I just wanted to make Jack Muldowney mad. We'd been dating for about a year. We'd had a falling out, and I wanted to make him jealous.

I was fifteen years old and working inside, on the counter, at a car hop restaurant called The Dutch Boy. It was the only place in Schenectady, New York, that had carhops, so it was a hangout frequented by car enthusiasts and hot rodders, most of whom were members of a car club called the Road Kings. The guys wore black satin jackets, with gold king's crowns embroidered on the back, jeans and white T-shirts. Quite a contrast from the little yellow and blue uniforms that the girls wore.

Nineteen year-old Jack Muldowney was a member of the Road Kings and he came by every night religiously. Everybody did. Nine, ten o'clock, they'd drop by, drink cokes, eat hamburgers. Leave, come back. Leave, come back. That sort of thing.

Jack was a nice-looking guy. Blond hair, Irish, blue eyes, very good with his hands... I mean, in terms of fabricating components for cars. It was serious business with them. He not only was a mechanic at trade, he also built and constructed hot rod cars. In the fifties, that was big time. It was wild! Everything was all out.

Jack had a '32 Ford coupe, chopped and channeled, with fenders that wrapped around the top of the tire and moved with the front wheels like motorcycle fenders. Very custom. It had a Mercury engine in it that would give you a heck of a ride, if that's what you were into. Which I was.

Jack graduated to a '51 Mercury which he customized. He taught me how to drive the Merc and we went street racing together. That was our form of recreation, every night after work, on our very short dates.

One night, Jack and I had this big fight and decided to go our separate ways. "Fine," I thought, "I'll show you what you're missing." And I set my sights on this twenty-year-old collegiate type with probably the nicest car on the block at that time. I *knew* that car would break Jack's back.

It was a *new* '56 Chevrolet and it was considered a REAL strong car. And NO ONE had a brand-new car that was the hot setup at that time! Evidently, this fellow's parents had deep pockets. With that car, he more or less pushed his way into the group.

It was Friday night. It was the heat of the summer. Everybody was hanging outside. Windows were down. Tops were down. I left work a half hour early, waving cheerfully "See you later, everybody!" with a look on my face like the cat that ate the mouse. Everybody, all the girls, knew what was going on, so when the collegiate guy and I walked out of the Dutch Boy, all of the Road Kings were standing there, including Jack.

We got into the front seat of this fellow's '56 Chevy and I moved real close to him so that Jack could see me. My date started the car and quickly backed out of the driveway of the Dutch Boy, made a U-turn around the island in the middle of the divided highway, and took off in low gear.

If you have any idea what the cars were like in the fifties, you know they ran pretty fast. They had no restrictions on them, no emissions control, nothing.

So we went down this two-lane highway and he wound the car out and got as much as he could out of low gear, and very expert, he went for second gear. The thing was absolutely peaked out at 6500 RPMs and he *totally missed* second gear. It was terrible! You could hear it all the way in Scotia, New York, and *everyone* could see it.

I turned around and looked back at the Dutch Boy and it was awful: at least thirty car enthusiasts were jumping up and down laughing at us, rolling on the ground, cackling. Thank God, I wasn't driving! But it was still one of the most embarrassing moments in my life. I didn't even have the nerve to go back to the group and say I'd left with the wrong guy. And my date was too embarrassed to speak to me as he drove home.

The next day, Jack came by the Dutch Boy during his lunch hour. We struck up a conversation, and after that, I never went out with the Chevy owner again. I don't remember him coming to the Dutch Boy either. Because the real racers, well, they laughed him down pretty badly; I think it was hard for the guy to take.

The guy with the Chevy wasn't a bad guy, but he wasn't my cup of tea, either. I was just using him to make Jack mad, and I guess it did the trick. Because, by the end of 1956, Jack and I got married.

LeRoy Neiman

ANDREA BRAZZI

Action artist LeRoy Neiman has painted Muhammed Ali, Jack Nicklaus, Bobby Hull, Chris Evert, entertainers, celebrities, world leaders, Olympic athletes, Las Vegas gamblers and racetrack railbirds. He has also contributed humorous sketches to *Playboy* magazine monthly since 1955.

I asked this very attractive young lady to accompany me to *the* annual charity party in Denver. This is not one of those New York or Washington parties where people stop in for a few minutes along their evening's social route. People go out of their way to get to this lavish and exclusive weekend event.

Everyone was there: Sinatra, a lot of movie stars, and many other "A" list people from all fields who were certainly worth talking to. My date didn't know a person in the room.

While chatting in an intimate group which included an ex-President of the U.S. and his First Lady (who was talking about her recent surgery experience), I turned to my date for a positive reaction to a meaningful statement I had just made and discovered she was no longer at my side. The group also made note of her departure. It wasn't as if she paced the conversation; these people just weren't used to being abandoned by anybody.

Holding position, I kept an eye out for just where my date had wandered, giving her the benefit of the doubt that she might have taken a powder in the ladies' room.

Eventually, I spotted the truant prominently positioned on the other side of the room in a tight group circling Henry Kissinger. She was animatedly rapping with the renowned international figure.

At the right moment, I excused myself from the group and proceeded directly to Kissinger's coterie to reclaim my date. When I asked her why she had rudely slipped off, she justified the move by saying, "After all, Henry is the top man in the room, isn't he?"

I wasn't angry. I just figured I now knew my companion.

David Nuell

David Nuell is executive producer of *Entertainment Tonight* and *Entertainment This Week.* Prior to *ET*, he was an Emmy Award-winning station manager/news director for WRC-TV in Washington.

CHIP STONE

I'm not a real man of the world. Sharing popcorn at the movies is a big thing for me.

Actually, I'm very much of a romantic, I love a fire in the fireplace, soft music, candles and some nice wine. When I was in college in the early sixties, I even took rowboat picnics. I took Penny, a girl I'd met at a tea at a nearby girls school, on such a boat ride when I was eighteen or nineteen. She was charmed.

I thought Penny was the most beautiful girl I had ever seen. She was from Michigan, which, to a guy who grew up in Missouri and was away from home for the first time, made her seem worldly and fascinating. (Of course, you'd have to have grown up in Missouri to understand how fascinating someone from Michigan could be... Still, I thought she was charming.)

For about a semester, I took this vivacious, dark-haired drama major on many innocent and proper dates. I certainly wasn't pinned to her or anything. It was just one of those wonderful, post-adolescent, puppy-love romances.

From time to time, I heard a rumor that Penny was involved sexually with my roommate and certain other people on campus. I knew my roommate would have sex with anyone who would stand still. In fact, he actually enrolled in a girls' college as a ballet student, although he wasn't a dancer, in order to get access to a supply of young women. Therefore, anything I heard about him was certainly possible. But with Penny, I could never bring myself to believe any of that or discuss it with him. I didn't want to know.

Penny and I drifted apart, as happens with puppy-lovers, and I went about my career. Approximately fifteen years later, I was introduced to a man who subsequently became a long-term co-worker in producing television shows. We had totally different backgrounds: he was from Michigan, I was from Missouri. We went to different universities, took different courses. He worked for ABC; I worked for NBC. We were finally brought together in Washington, D.C., and began working in a very successful professional relationship.

In the course of getting to know him, I mentioned the fact that while in college I had met a young woman from his hometown and she was one of the most wonderful girls I had ever dated. He asked her name, and when I told him, he said, "Oh, well, you must have had a pretty good time because everyone in high school was hitting her." Even him.

He said she was one of those "always available good-time girls" who the Michigan boys were very sorry to see go off to Missouri. So much for puppy-love and innocent romance.

Even though so much time had passed, I felt so embarrassed by this revelation that I think my face flushed. It cut to the very core of my manliness, because from the way he talked, I was the *only person* who never scored with this girl. So, fifteen years later, it turned out that I had not one, but a whole semester full of bad dates.

I've rationalized it now by saying our relationship was on a higher plane than hot, sweaty, passionate, tawdry sex. Maybe it was true puppy-love after all.

Bill O'Reilly

Now host of *Inside Edition*, Bill O'Reilly was previously a network correspondent for ABC's *World News Tonight with Peter Jennings*. O'Reilly has been a columnist for *Boston Herald* since 1985.

The American Cancer Society sponsored a benefit where they auctioned off twelve bachelors in tuxes to two hundred ladies from Brooklyn. It was like a casbah, standing up there. The bidding started and I was bought by an attractive professional in her mid-thirties for $500, which in Brooklyn is pretty big bucks. I was happy with the outcome because the other two contenders looked like they had just gotten out on parole.

The deal was, the bachelors paid for the date. I figured since this lady had spent a lot of money nailing me, I'd better take her to a pretty nice restaurant in New York City.

Halfway through the meal the girl started asking me questions like, "Are you going out with anybody else? What are your plans for the future? What do you like to see in women?" Really, really honing in on the big issues. I was fending off most of them with a combination of jokes and honesty, until she asked, "What do you think of monogamy?"

I could have looked over my shoulder and said, "Are you talkin' to me?" but I thought this might not be the right thing to say to an obviously serious woman. My humor got me through dinner and several other pointed inquiries about family and children, but I was still quite confused.

When I took her back to her place, she asked me if I wanted to come up. I said, "No, I didn't wanna do that on the first date." I mean, she was well-educated and had a nice body but I felt uncomfortable about her aggressive behavior.

No was not the answer she was looking for.

"Look, Bill," she said, "I'm *very* interested in you, and I really want to continue this *relationship.*"

Relationship? I know it's the modern age and everything, but we'd only spent a few hours together. Maybe she assumed she knew me because she watched my show? I didn't want to stay to find out.

About three days later, I was curious about this odd experience, and since she was a good-looking woman who dressed very provocatively, I decided to give her a call. She was very angry when she got on the line. "Well, why didn't you call the next day?" she demanded.

"I was busy. I was under water like I usually am. You know my show."

"Well, you should have called me the next day. It was terribly rude of you. That's no way to begin a *relationship.*"

That word again! I backed away real fast because I now had intense visions of *Play Misty for Me.*

When I described this experience to a woman who's a friend of mine, she burst out laughing. "Oh, well, she read the book."

"What book?"

"How to Find the Perfect Mate in a Year or Your Money Back."

"How much money?"

"Five hundred bucks."

I'd never heard of it, but apparently there's a $500 book which tells women to go right after a guy they think is a potential mate, find out everything about him as quickly as possible, and then declare their objectives, immediately.

I sure hope this lady got a refund. If she didn't, I was certainly a very expensive bad date.

Lou Diamond Phillips

Since his debut in *La Bamba*, Lou Diamond Phillips has starred in a series of diverse films including *Stand and Deliver*, *Young Guns*, *Disorganized Crime*, *Renegades*, *The First Power* and *Show of Force*.

I had this car I called "The Green Hornet." It was actually an Opal Manta that my grandfather had given me for my sixteenth birthday. He was a used-car salesman and he probably couldn't sell it.

Sometimes this Hornet would not go into second gear—you know, you'd be driving down the freeway and it wouldn't downshift and you'd be caught in neutral going fifty miles an hour. I could handle it. But it was, unfortunately, the only way I had of getting my sweet, unassuming, fifteen-year-old date to see *Superman*.

I ended up getting a late start. Naturally, the Hornet had some trouble. We were barely going to make the beginning of the movie and I ran out of gas. She looked at me as if to say, "We just left. Are you trying something already?"

At the time I was kind of a "big-man-on-campus" (class president for three years, key club, athlete, lots of other activities), but I was never a Don Juan. (That would have been too much responsibility.) However, I was sixteen, so I naturally would have wanted to try something a little later. "No," I confessed, "I'm *really* out of gas. I was in such a hurry I forgot to put gas in the car."

I pushed the car two miles to a gas station. She drove.

Two miles! It looked sooo close. But in Corpus Christi, Texas, *everything* is completely flat. I could see the lights of the station, but by the time I finished pushing the car, it seemed like a lot longer than two miles.

Wonderful start.

We got five bucks of gas and drove to the theatre. The first showing of *Superman* had begun and we were an hour early for the second showing. Since I only had fifteen bucks left in my pocket, I knew I couldn't ask her to get something to eat while we waited for the show, because I also knew I needed eight bucks for two movie tickets and two bucks for popcorn and coke. We were stuck there.

She called her folks and told them she'd be in later than she thought, which was past both our midnight curfews.

We saw *Superman*. Everything was wonderful. We get out, get into the car, start to pull out of the parking lot and I get a flat tire. It's almost midnight. Everyone's honking and shouting, I don't have a spare, and I'm thinking, Christopher Reeves I am not. So...

I pushed the car *another two miles* to *another* gas station. She drove.

I spend my last five bucks to have the tire filled and patched, while she sits there patiently and waits. At least she's polite enough not to call her father and have him come pick her up. That would have added insult to injury. Which I certainly didn't need at that point.

Meanwhile, I'm wondering, what else will go wrong? Will someone hit my car on the way home? Will my dad take away the keys because I missed my curfew?

About one o'clock in the morning (on a school night!), I got her home. By that time, any passion that was there was gone, deflated like the tire. Devastated and embarrassed, I left without even trying for a goodnight kiss.

Two days later, I laughed about it and chalked it up to my inexperience as a "Superhero."

Paula Poundstone

ANNE FISHBEIN

Discovered by Robin Williams, Paula Poundstone was named Best Female Comedy Club Stand-Up at the Third Annual American Comedy Awards. She has appeared on *The Tonight Show*, *Late Night with David Letterman*, HBO's *Young Comedians*, A&E's *Evening at the Improv*, and other programs for network and cable.

People tend to say the worst things to me. One time I was at this Beverly Hills restaurant with this guy. At the beginning of the meal, they served some bread and soup, and we ate that, and he had some appetizer that I maybe tasted, and maybe I had some soup myself. Then the entrée came and I didn't really like it, so I hardly ate any of it. I swear the busboy cleared a practically full plate. Then I asked the waitress if I could see a dessert menu and she looked right at me and said, "You know, I've never seen anyone eat this much."

I'm not a person who cares that much about that sort of thing, but it was a funny thing to say to a person who's like a woman-with-a-guy on sort-of-a-date. So I said to the waitress, "Hold the menu," and we left for Baskin Robbins.

Then another time I went out with this guy, and we were out shopping for an alarm clock about 2:30 in the morning. It was after a show, we're both comics, and I needed an alarm clock because I had to get up on time the next morning and I had no way of doing that.

So we're talking and I said to him, "I don't date because I don't like sex."

I know it's an odd thing to say, and I think it's even odder that no matter who I go out with, they always say the exact same thing, which is, when I tell them that I don't like sex, they always say, "Well, you'll like it with me." Then I say, "Well, have I inadvertently gone out with Sam I Am? I don't like sex, I don't. I do not like it in a house, I do not like it with a mouse."

At the end of the evening, for some odd reason, this guy had this transformation where I think he did indeed decide that he wanted something of the sexual nature. I repeated that although I enjoyed a man's company, I did not particularly want a big sexual situation.

He said, "Well, you know, Paula, a lot of guys think you're gay." I don't know if that was supposed to be a compelling reason for me to sleep with him. I guess he somehow thought that if I slept with him, he would sign an affidavit and show it to the fellows so that they would indeed know that I was obviously able to participate.

I still said no. That's a pretty bad date.

Soon after, he heard me tell the story on stage. He knew it was him and was fairly surprised that my position got such a strong positive reaction from the crowd.

Terry Power

CHIP STONE

Terry Power is a film and music video producer with a strong religious upbringing who has worked extensively with MC Hammer, Tone-Loc and other rap artists.

Terry Power cruises with performers
Good & Plenty

I was housesitting in an upper-class bedroom community, where I had this incredible arrangement—a beautiful house, XKE Jaguar at my disposal, and a swimming pool. All I had to do was take care of the family dog, make sure the house was safe while the people were away in Europe, and keep an eye on my housemate, Sophie, an older woman whose husband had run off with the high school home-ec teacher, who had taught all of her five children. This drove her to drink.

I never saw Sophie eat a meal. All I saw her consume was vodka, Triscuits and Cheez Whiz. That was it.

Sophie was desperate to set me up with this girl down the street. I continually said, "Look, Sophie, I'm not interested. I'll meet somebody, I'm sure."

But she kept after me to see this girl. "She's a lovely girl. You'll hit it off. You'll have a great time."

Finally, one weekend, I came home from my job search and she said, "Terry, I know you didn't want me to do this, but I set up the date for you. You have a date with this girl tonight." I thought, Oh, God, okay... How bad could it be?

I go pick up this girl at her place. First thing she tells me, she's leaving town the next day. I say, "Sooo, this is your last night in town, Susan, we should have a good time. Where are you going?"

"Virginia," she says casually.

"God, Virginia! What's down there?" I was truly surprised.

"I'm entering a convent," she answers flatly.

The woman was entering A NUNNERY the very next day! Only a drunk could get something that wrong!

We go to a movie. Have an uneventful dinner afterwards. And as I lean over to kiss her goodnight, I jokingly say, "Sooo, you're leaving for the convent tomorrow. Want to see God a day early?"

She slugged me.

I think she really was a virgin. Because four summers later, I bumped into her at a Fourth of July parade, and she ran up to me screaming gleefully, "Terry, Terry, I'm out! I'm out!" At this rate, I expect I'll see her next in *Playboy* magazine, with the confessional, "I Was Once a NUN!"

Vincent Price

Vincent Price has appeared in hundreds of productions for stage, film, television (both network and public), and radio. His one-man show on Oscar Wilde has toured internationally.

This was a date with a girl who has been my dear friend for all these many years. The date cemented our friendship, but ruined our budding romance.

I was fourteen. She was fourteen. It was our first big date.

I decided to take her to the "hard ticket" movie, which, in those days was the more expensive road show. I chose the picture because it starred my favorite actor, one who I was to work with on his last two pictures many years later. The road-show film was *Beau Geste*, and the actor was Ronald Colman.

She got all dolled up. Put on a little mascara, which was very risqué for a fourteen-year-old girl at the time. And we went out to the movies. She had beautiful eyes...but the mascara added a little mystery and romance.

As we watched the picture, we held hands discreetly, which was about as far as you could go on a first date in those days.

At one point during the picture, I turned to her hoping for a grateful peck on the cheek. She was sobbing. It was the most tragic moment...the mascara was striped down her cheeks.

I felt like sobbing too, but for a different reason.

She was so embarrassed, I took her right home. And there she left me, out in the cold, as she had to get the mascara off before her mother caught her.

That was it... my great romantic date. There was one consolation—movie seats were under a dollar then, and popcorn was a quarter.

We never had another date. But she's been my friend for all these years... and friends are sometimes harder to hold on to.

Rain Pryor

Rain Pryor plays the streetwise T.J. on the TV series, *Head of the Class*. Rain began her acting career at twelve in the West Coast Production of *Runaways* and appeared in the twentieth anniversary production of *Hair*.

He and his roommate stole the garden hose from the neighbor's house and were attaching it to the faucet when my girlfriend and I walked in. I hadn't seen him since I went out with him at Camp Interlocken when we were twelve. He was a babe then, he was a major babe now. My girlfriend came along to be with his friend.

"Let me fill up my waterbed, okay?" he said.

"Now?"

I was kinda disappointed this was the first thing he said to two girls who were, like, dressed decent, with makeup on and everything. But what was I gonna do? They'd just moved to town and he needed something to sleep on. "Oh, well," I said. "Let's wait."

"No, no, no, it's gonna take four hours, okay. We'll go eat, come back and it'll be done. Then we'll go to the movies."

He assumed it would take four hours to fill up because back home in Michigan when he had drained the bed out, the draining took four hours. But he didn't have the directions. He'd lost them in the move. I was, like, you're a geek. But, you know, it's not my king-size waterbed.

So, we go to eat at this place right down the street from their house and we come back and the bed is, like, up to the ceiling. You know in cartoons, when they show something about to explode and it's like huger than life? That's what this bed looked like.

It was like 5'3" high with water, I swear. It was so big it was starting to get stretch marks and the frame was already on the floor. I sat there and I looked and had to look again, 'cause I'm thinking, This is not happening, you know.

He goes, "Let's just try to drain it out, and then we'll go to the movies."

We worked on it for at least three hours, taking turns with the hose, blowing and sucking, blowing and sucking. Some water would rush out. The bed went down a little bit, but we all were dying. Finally, we're like, "Wait, there has to be another solution."

So my date says, "Maybe if I make a hole with a pin, the water will come out easier?"

Well, he makes a hole in the water bed, and BOOM! The bed explodes. It's like a tidal wave all over the apartment. Every room is covered—the bedrooms, the two bathrooms, living room, dining room, breakfast nook, everything. This place was on the first floor so the water leaked into *all* the apartments on the side and also into the garage.

His friend was thrown against the wall. For a minute there I thought I was gonna drown—even though I was on my high school swim team.

My high-heeled, black satin shoes turned color, cause the paint wasn't dry on 'em yet. I'd just bought 'em. And, god, my hair was a mess.

My girlfriend's going, "If we add some soap, we could have bubble bath!"

We spent the rest of the evening trying to drain out the place with a line of garbage cans going from the bathroom to the bedroom.

They told the landlord it was the pipes, then quickly got rid of the bed. As far as I know, they're still sleeping on the floor.

Ann Richards

SCOTT NEWTON

Ann Richards stirred millions of Americans with her keynote speech at the 1988 Democratic Convention. State treasurer of Texas since 1982, she is preparing to run for the office of governor. Richards is the first woman to be elected to a statewide office in Texas in over fifty years.

My parents were protective, to say the least. I was an only child and they just thought they needed to keep me from being exposed to the wild world of men. It was probably just as well, because my first date was undoubtedly the worst date I have *ever* had.

There was this very sophisticated boy in my class at high school in Waco, Texas, named Buddy. I don't have any idea why he chose me, but out of the blue, he invited me to go as his date to this annual, fancy-dress, wintertime dance called the De Molay Dance. The De Molay is sort of an adjunct to the Masonic Lodge for young high school boys.

The dance was held at a big hotel or a Masonic Lodge. I'm not real positive, I *only* remember the marble floor.

I didn't travel in the social circles where one would go to debutante parties and stuff like that. I was also younger than most of the kids in my grade at school (about fourteen when I was in eleventh grade), so going to this dance was really a pretty big deal for me.

There were, however, several immediate and pressing problems. First of all, I didn't know what I was going to do about getting permission to go to this thing until finally some of my girlfriends talked my parents into allowing me to have a "car date" with this boy. Then, I didn't have a formal dress to wear and my parents didn't have the wherewithal to pull together the money to buy one. We borrowed a dress from somebody; I can't even remember who it was.

It was uuugggly!! It was a striped taffeta dress and it really didn't fit me very well. A bit big! I don't even know how old the thing was, but it was certainly not a stylish dress!

And I didn't have any shoes, so I had to wear a pair of summer thong sandals with the taffeta dress.

And it was winter, and I had to have a coat.

My aunt had a fur coat. It was probably skunk. Totally inappropriate and kind of overwhelming. But I wore it, along with the taffeta dress and the summer thong sandals.

So we got me all gussied up in this borrowed rig and I was a nervous wreck. I was not only nervous about actually having a date—what to say and how to talk—but I felt like I just looked like a frump. Especially when my date came to the door in his tux!

AND...I didn't know how to dance!!!

We got to the dance and I was stepping all over the dress and the boy. After about an hour, we got into a line to get some punch and I promptly threw up all over the dress, the boy, the girl in front of me, AND the *marble* floor. It was that cheap little gray stuff, and the worst part is, when anything hits it, it *splats!*

I just cannot tell you how bad it was.

I ran off to the bathroom. He ran off to the bathroom. I was such a mess, I didn't know if I was really sick or a bundle of nerves. In the bathroom, I wiped as much off the dress as I could, but obviously I had to go home.

Well, this boy I was with was terribly sophisticated and smoked cigarettes, and we were double-dating with a couple, and she was the most beautiful senior girl in the high school, so, of course, it couldn't have been worse.

The four of us got in the car to take me home. The heater was on, and the boy was smoking his cigarettes, and naturally all the windows were rolled up because it was winter, and the odor of this dress permeated everything in that car. I knew, from that moment, that my life was ruined. That never again would I get to go anywhere. That the fame of my indiscretion in vomiting all over a date at a dance would spread all through the high school. (Which it did.) And it was, without doubt, the most devastating period of my life.

I swear my parents knew something dreadful was going to happen because when I walked in the door, I found them pacing the floor. They were surely doing this from the moment I left, knowing that I was probably killed on the way to the thing. At that point, that might have been better than how I felt. But I must say, it didn't hurt my life—although I certainly will never forget the experience!

My date was actually very nice to me about the whole matter and even asked me to go somewhere else real soon. I never accepted his polite invitation. I was just too embarrassed, and, of course, the lid was back on at home.

I learned from that, though. Now I'm always very cautious about eating before anything that I consider a big deal.

Julia Roberts

JONATHAN LENNARD

Golden Globe-winning actress Julia Roberts credits include *Mystic Pizza*, *Steel Magnolias* and *Pretty Woman*. She next stars with Kiefer Sutherland in *Flatliners*.

At thirteen, I was the first in my clique of girls from Smyrna, Georgia, to have an official date. With this I had taken on, unbeknownst to me, a huge responsibility.

I do not even know if I really liked him, but he was older—a senior. That seemed to be enough, at least for the clique. I spent a Saturday at the Center Mall looking for a shirt with stripes. He liked stripes—or so Katie Nicks had found out. And Katie, having the biggest, well, largest...I don't know, let's just say she had access to the most information.

When finally evening descended upon our fair town, the doorbell rang. All eyes turned to me. Excitement filled my body. Maturity was here, or so it seemed, and I was going to throw up. I ran to the bathroom and begged my mother to send him away. She did not. We left my house together.

We walked the length of the driveway, reaching the chariot that was to carry me to womanhood—an El Camino. An El Camino? Half car, half truck; the automobile of indecision. This couldn't possibly be my transport to adulthood. Well, it was.

The date began with a movie. An hour and forty minutes filled with the madcap adventures of several hundred midgets. He howled with continuous laughter. I did not. Finally, the credits rolled and we were off to eat at a place called the Mellow Mushroom.

The restaurant was filled with smoke and leftover beatniks, which, at the time, I was too young to appreciate. I decided, however, that it was "groovy" of this boy to have sought out such an interesting place to take me. It showed imagination, a sense of adventure, and mind enough to venture out of our town limits. This was impressive.

Upon inquiring how he'd come to know of this place, all these ideas were put to rest. The adventurous, free spirit I had created in my mind had simply won a free pizza from a local radio station. He didn't even like this restaurant, said the people there gave him the creeps. So we ate our dinner in the car.

Maybe it was the mushrooms, or perhaps he had been feeling poorly all along. Suddenly there was this smell, not a pizza smell, no—this was a human smell. Another whiff, yes, definitely human. My mind began to race for the source. My eyes began to water from the pungent fumes. I wanted to laugh. I suppressed the urge to turn green. My date has gas! My date is actually farting! This was never mentioned in my Dating Years class. Do I run? No, no, a mature woman never runs. Remain calm. What would my sister Lisa do? Be polite. I choked out one last plea—"Excuse me, could we please open a window?"

With amazing nonchalance, he rolled the window down, only to immediately turn his attention back to the pizza. I looked at him hard as if to ask: Are you okay? Don't you smell it? Did something die inside you? He looked into my questioning eyes equally hard and chirped "Fine weather we're having, huh? Want something else to drink?"

Needing nothing more from this person, we left for home while I negotiated deals with the devil to be in a convertible. I passed the time wondering who this boy was next to me. Not the best athlete in the school, not the one whose name was called out by everyone in the halls, but a boring, smelly boy who obviously couldn't make up his mind whether he wanted a car or a truck, and who had tried to kill me and had almost succeeded.

As the car was still in motion in my driveway. I had already said thank you, goodnight, and was on my feet. But as I turned to go, he was in front of me wearing a strange look, this queer sort of smile I had only seen on *Love Boat*. We kissed. I felt I had to for him, for me, for curiosity's sake. Hell, I was doing it for everybody in Smyrna.

All in all, I felt nothing. He reacted a little differently— suddenly hands were flying, hair was pulled, and I realized: I am thirteen; I am bored; I do not like you; shit, I still pee in the bathtub; this is not something I am ready for.

It is funny, I had envisioned this date, this lead-in to dating, as something that was going to metamorphose me into a woman. Somehow the simple acting out of this ritual was going to change me, and I felt certain that by morning I would see the world through new eyes.

The stillness of the morning was broken by the shriek of the telephone demanding attention. My comrades called, breathless to know the answer to one burning question... "Did he kiss you?" My answer was a question burning in its own right... "What is all the fuss about? It was, after all, just a date."

So young, so jaded.

Rollins

Former leader of the punk band, Black Flag, Rollins currently fronts the Rollins Band. He affectionately refers to himself as the "unpoetical, unstoppable, lyrical bum, public enemy Number One."

TEXAS HOTEL RECORDS

I was going to this all-boys school and all I knew was guys and homework and gym. I did not know anything about women. I mean, I was a totally normal, fifteen-year-old male, who, every time he saw a girl went, "Yeah, this is hot! That is where I wanta be—up that girl's skirt!" but I was just terrified to talk to girls.

Somehow my friends convinced me to go out to a party where I didn't know a single person, except for the guys who I was with, and they were all off hanging out with all these girls. That left me standing there like a wax statue feeling really, really, REALLY bad.

I wanted to get outa there. Then suddenly this girl came over to me and she said, "Hi! What's your name?"

I said, "Henry."

She said, "I'm Ann."

I said, "Ohhhh wow... Hi!" I was just amazed a girl would talk to me.

Ann wasn't all that attractive to me: she was just a plain, fifteen, sixteen-year-old-looking girl, with a very round face and very oily skin, with some acne on it. She had blond-brown curly hair and was a bit overweight. Looks didn't matter. The fact that she was nice to me and talked to me did.

Driving back into town with my friends, I was all pumped up. I went, "Wow, man, I was just talking to this girl!" Everyone went, "Ohhh, yeah, that's Ann. Everyone knows her. She hangs out." I went, "Wow, what's her phone number?" They went, "Noooo, come ooonnn. Don't ask HER out." I said, "Ohhh, I think she's pretty cool, don't you?"

I couldn't get anyone to agree with me. But I finally managed to get her number from one of these guys. Then it took me three or four days to screw up the courage and call her and ask, "Uhhh, do you want to go out?" She didn't seem all that into it, but she still went, "Yeah... okay."

At school the next day I said to my buddies, "You are not going to believe this, *I* am going out on a date." They said, "Nooo, YOU'RE not going on *a date?!* You?"

All these people thought I was the school freak because they were into eight-track tapes, Trans-Ams, scamming their fathers' credit cards, drinking too many Michelobs and I was into having a real job (I worked at a pet store), reading books, listening to Ted Nugent and soul music, and taking care of my snakes and my tarantula.

The plan was: I was going to meet the girl for dinner Friday evening at the Zebra Room on Wisconsin Avenue, a pizza and beer type place. No big deal. Good food, though. Then we were going to go to a school dance at this other school in town.

I was totally inexperienced. But on television, when you take a girl out, you get flowers, so I figured, hey, get some flowers. Friday afternoon, I went to Pete the Flower Man and just said, "Pete, I am going out on a date." He said, "I can't believe it. YOU are going out on a date?" And he gave me some flowers.

I met her at the Zebra, and I gave her these flowers, and I said, "Here, I got these for you." She looked at them funny and said, "Ohhh... thanks," and put them down. I thought, God, I should probably get out of here.

We ordered some food and talked about some stupid shit, like,

"Ohhh, how's your history class?" I tried to make the best of it and hoped she wouldn't go away.

Then we went to this dance. As soon as we got there, she took off and I was just standing there going, "Oh, God!"

She came back and said, "Look...ahhh...my friends are here...and...ummmm, look, ahhh...the only reason I came up and talked to you the other night at that party was your friends came over and said you were shy and you needed someone to talk to...I really didn't want to go out with you...I have a boyfriend and if he finds out that I was hanging out with you, he will be very angry, and I didn't really want to go out with you at all...I was kinda afraid to say no...so—I'm sorry. Have a nice night." Then she shook my hand and she disappeared.

I didn't run home and slash my wrists, but it sure felt like it would if you walked out on stage at the Forum and the curtain opened and the place was sold out and you forgot your PANTS! Really, it blew me away! It made me feel bad for desiring to be with someone, and totally embarrassed, when I didn't do anything wrong at all: a girl was nice to me, so I asked her out. I mean, I didn't shoot her!

If it had already happened to me five times, I could've just laughed about it. But it hadn't, so I bawled. I walked outside and sat on this bench in the dark. Then this other girl came up to me, sat down and went, "Hi." I didn't have anything to say to her but by then I was so mad, I could talk.

She said, "What's your name?"

"Henry." And I thought, Here we go again.

She said, "You want a cigarette?"

I didn't smoke. But I went, "Yeah...sure!"

She handed me this cigarette and I put it in my mouth, she handed me a lighter and I lit up. She was smoking, and I was trying to smoke. But I couldn't get any air through the cigarette and I thought, What's the matter with this goddamn cigarette? Then, because it was dark, I put the cigarette up against the sky where there was a little bit of moonlight and I saw I had lit the filter end.

I figured I would just call it a night. I said, "Hey, I gotta go," threw the cigarette on the ground and split.

I walked all the way home, feeling pretty small. Always makes me think of the cover of that Frank Sinatra LP *In the Wee Small Hours*.

Monday my buddies at school said, "Well, how was the date? Of course I lied, "Dumped her." They went, "Yeah, right!" (You know what fifteen-year-old jerks do.) Finally I said, "Well, she had this boyfriend . . ." They said, "That's why we were telling you, DON'T GO OUT WITH HER! She's just a friend, you know. You don't ask out every girl that talks to you."

I learned all that shit the hard way.

That date kept me in my basement, away from girls for the next eight months. When I emerged, I was totally hot to get laid. And since then I have cut a path littered with panties, broken hearts, and tears. Haw! Haw! Haw! Not really, but I still listen to Ted Nugent, a true prophet.

Pete Rozelle

Commissioner of the National Football League from 1960 to 1989, Pete Rozelle has been involved with the promotion of sports since his high school days in Lynwood, California. He was both publicity director and general manager for the Los Angeles Rams and was a partner in an international public relations firm.

I knocked out my two front teeth on my first fall at an ice skating party. I was fourteen-years old when it happened and had succumbed to the peer pressure to learn to skate.

The dentist told me not to worry. He'd fitted me with a partial, temporary plate that hooked onto my back teeth and looked pretty good. Although I was supposed to take it out occasionally for cleaning, it was intended to stay put until I was old enough to get a permanent bridge.

About a year after this, I was at a small party at this gal's house and a very mature fifteen-year-old girl picked me for post office. I don't know if you remember how to play the game, but one person says, "I'm the postman and I have a letter for" whoever they want and that person has to pay for that letter by going off to a closet or some other room and kissing the mail carrier. Then the kisser becomes the carrier and so on.

So, I'm in a darkened closet with this gal and she was a very hard kisser. After about ninety seconds of this aggressive smooching, my temporary plate flipped loose in my mouth. Rather than choke, I tried to tongue it back into position, while continuing to gracefully complete the kiss.

It didn't work all that well, so within fifteen seconds, I excused myself to the bathroom. Thoroughly embarassed, I quickly adjusted the plate and refrained from kissing girls for about a year and a half. By then I'd gotten my courage up and was able to handle the soft kissers in private.

Still, the fear of a public slipup kept me away from kissing parties for several more years—until I got my permanent bridge.

Ed Ruscha

Internationally acclaimed artist Ed Ruscha is noted for, among other things, his sly sayings on canvas. Ruscha's work is in the permanent collection of museums including the Whitney Museum of American Art, Los Angeles County Museum of Art and Hischorn Museum & Sculpture Gallery.

I had a bad date in Indio once about three years ago. It was my own fault because I had been driving nonstop from Phoenix and just went for the first one I saw. My stomach was sore for days.

Or here's a bad date that's a nondate.

I have an old friend named Bill Elder. A school chum of mine from Oklahoma that I just thought had dropped out of sight for good. I didn't know where he was living. I completely forgot about him.

Twenty-six years later I saw him on the street in Los Angeles.

I pulled up to the curb and immediately recognized him. Actually, I had time to recognize him because there was a stop sign. He recognized me, through the windshield, from about one-hundred feet away.

Then he just marched right up to my car, like he was belligerent and exasperated, and said, "Well, it's about time you got here!"

Just having him do that was so hilarious to me that now, whenever I run into somebody by accident, I always use the same approach.

We sat and we chatted. It was like great old times.

I haven't seen him again. We didn't even exchange numbers.

Jane Russell

Jane Russell's big break came when she auditioned for Howard Hughes in his nationwide "chest hunt" for his movie *The Outlaw*. From there, Jane Russell's cleavage became a household topic. She has made dozens of films, including *Gentlemen Prefer Blondes*, *Paleface*, *Born Losers* and *Foxfire*.

When I was fifteen, I would have given my eye teeth for a ride on one of the speed boats at Lake Arrowhead.

Every day that summer, I would stand on the pier, hoping that one of the gang of rich kids, who were all about my age, would come by and ask me to join them. They all seemed like nice American kids from a distance; they were just living a life beyond my means.

One day, this young guy who owned one of the boats pulled up to the pier and asked me to hop aboard. We sped about a bit and then he asked me for a date later that day. He said he was having a little party at his parents' house, which was an enormous cabin on the island in the middle of the lake, and arranged to pick me up in his boat at the pier.

At the time, I was staying with a friend of my mother's, taking care of her while she nursed a broken leg. This woman lived way up the side of the mountain in a cabin, tucked into the pine trees, that took miles to reach by car.

Two or three boatloads of kids arrived at the island about the same time. Among the crowd was Bill Holden. I didn't remember this, but he told me years later, that he too had been standing on the dock and was asked by a rich girl to come along with her to this party.

The maid and butler were waiting for my date as he came through the door, counted us, and announced, "There'll be eighteen of us for lunch." Then he strode into the game room where there were pool tables and whatnot. I dropped my teeth. Eighteen for lunch? No one said those kinds of things at Van Nuys High School.

My date turned on the radio and started playing pool. People followed his lead, and we did that until the maid came to the door and said, "Lunch is served." After that, because his parents weren't around, we had the run of the house and grounds for hours.

About eleven at night it was time to go. We took the boat back to the pier and on the way I started to wonder how we were going to get back up the mountain to the cabin. I guess I thought there would be a car or he would get one or something. I was wearing high heels and a white dress with a red zipper down the front, all the way down. I never considered climbing a mountain.

But when we got to the other side, there was no car. It was pitch dark. In other words, there was no choice but to start trudging up the long winding road to the cabin. As we were climbing, I suddenly realized that if we went straight through the brush, instead of following the curves in the road, it would be quicker.

It was rough going, there were lots of thorns and long branches and pine needles. We were both getting scratched and dirty and soon my date started to complain, "Oh, Jeez, well, how much further is it? I can't deal with this. I think I'd better go back."

That's exactly what he did. He left me there—a fifteen-year-old girl in a white dress with high heels—to climb a mountain of brumble by herself at midnight. It was terrifying, shocking and infuriating: most of the boys from Van Nuys High School would have seen to it that I got home safely, but this was too much for the rich kid.

That was my first experience with spoiled young men. From then on, I checked to see if my suitors were gentlemen, or at least got to know them a little bit better before I went out.

Kimberly Russell

Best known for her regular role of Sarah Nevins on the TV series, *Head of the Class*, Kimberly Russell soon stars opposite Bill Cosby in *Ghost Dad*. Her theater credits include *Beyond Your Command* and *Black Girl*.

His name was Stanley. He wore thick, horn-rimmed glasses, and whenever he would stop by my dressing room, he would talk about French literature and poetry. He loved the fact that French literature wasn't just a story, that the "art of it" was the words themselves and the way the sentences were beautifully formed.

He reminded me of Woody Allen. But I would say he was a worse version.

When he arrived at my door for our date, he was wearing loafers and mustard-colored pants that were worn in the knees. His shirt had every color in the rainbow mixed in a plaid, and with it he wore a paisley tie. His thick, black hair, as usual, was parted on one side and all combed over to the other side. He wasn't trying to be hip. That was just his playwright style.

I remember I did some investigation. He told me he was from New York and it turned out that he was from Hoboken. I wondered why he was covering up, but I didn't ask. All I knew was that he was anxious to take me to this little restaurant in the Village called Tex-Mex.

The moment we walked in the restaurant, he said, "I'll order for you." I said, "Okay, fine." He had been there before. It was obvious.

As soon as the waiter came over, he said, "We will have pork chops, we will have the mashed potatoes, and, oh, yeah, we will order squash and apple pie." There were no appetizers. No soft drinks beforehand. Just boom, boom, boom. I think he must have wanted me to think he was in control because I'd never seen him so macho.

Then he said, "Kimberly, you know what I love about you?"

"What?"

"Your scent. I really love your scent."

I thought, Oh, my god!!! I knew I shouldn't trust a guy who left flowers and charming notes in my dressing room. But within seconds, he turned the line around, and I thought, Okay, that's a nice compliment. Then he continued, "You know, Kimberly, you remind me of my aunt."

"Really?"

"Yes. She worked in a factory. I remember she would come home and she would smell like—well, there would be the mixture of her perspiration from having worked so hard and her perfume—and you smell... sort of like her." Then he pulled out his crumpled handkerchief and wiped his runny nose. "I have this allergy," he said, replacing the handkerchief, sniffing loudly, and digging into his pork chops.

He continued to wipe his nose throughout the dinner. I was so disgusted by the dripping that I didn't eat any of my food. When I say I didn't touch it, I didn't touch it. So when the waiter came to take our plates, he said, "Are you finished?"

I said, "Yes."

He said, "Ohhh, nononono. No! Keep her plate here. Keep the plate here because I want to *suck your bones.*"

The waiter looked at me with such pity, then walked away. I was just so embarrassed.

Stanley wasn't. He sat there and he ate every last bit of meat off those bones. And he sat there, and he sucked those bones.

I said, "Stanley, you really like those bones..."

"That's right. In my past life, I was a dog," he said earnestly as he scratched his ear. No wonder he liked my scent!

After dinner, he suggested that we go window-shopping in the East Village, where, we quickly discovered, every store was conveniently closed. This fact didn't stop him from pointing out the things he liked—particularly lingerie shops.

He had this fixation with anything snappable. Garters, things that hooked from one thing to another, things that were a unit. Especially in rose. "You would look so wonderful in rose, don't you think?"

"Stanley," I replied, "why are your hands so sweaty? Are you nervous?"

"No," he mumbled. "They are always sweaty."

"Well, I suggest you take baby powder and put it on your palms."

He assured me that he had tried that and it didn't work. But he thought this thing between us could, and wanted to set the next date.

"Stanley," I said, "remember what you said at dinner, about being a dog in your past life? Well, in my past life, I was a *cat*, and as far as I know, dogs and cats just don't get along."

"Really?" he chuckled.

"*Really.*"

I thanked him for the lovely evening, kissed him on the cheek, and let go of his hand. "Try the baby powder."

Fortunately, I caught a cab right there on the spot.

Meg Ryan

TIMOTHY WHITE/ONYX

Golden Globe nominee Meg Ryan has starred in eight feature films, including, *When Harry Met Sally, Joe Versus the Volcano* and *Promised Land.* She next stars opposite Val Kilmer in Oliver Stone's biography of Jim Morrison.

I just thought this guy was an artist. He was a freshman at college, he had a motorcycle, and he had these huge blue eyes and these long, gorgeous eyelashes. I still remember them. And Jackson Browne kind of hair. He just was my idea of the ultimate human being.

He comes up to my dorm and he picks me up on his motorcycle and he takes me for a nighttime winter ride through this beautiful landscape. We see cows. We go up and down these hills. It's northern Connecticut. We have this great time. Then we have a little picnic under the stars. It was just so wonderful.

He was a musician. So to me, he just personified all these great, really creative, I don't know, just neat things. 'Cause he wasn't a yuppie, you know. He was a romantic man. He dressed so neat. Everything about him was great.

After the picnic, he brings me back up to my dorm room and I just look at him. My heart is going. I mean, I was a freshman in college—I didn't know if I should kiss him. I didn't know what I should do.

Anyway, there was this great, intimate moment. He leans in and he kisses me, and then he says so sincerely, "I just had the greatest time, Meg."

"God, Bob, I did too. Thank you so much," and I went on and on.

His face just lost its elasticity. It looked like it just dropped to his knees. After a moment, he says flatly, "Okay, okay, all right." Then he leaves and drifts down the hall.

As he walks into the elevator, I remember that his name is *Bruce*. I just felt so awful.

I never saw him again. He was the ultimate, too.

Walter M. Schirra, Jr.

A graduate of the U.S. Naval Academy, Schirra became a top naval pilot before joining the NASA space program. He was involved in the Mercury, Gemini and Apollo projects. He is now a business executive.

I will relate one which didn't happen to me, but it happened to many of my contemporaries when I was a midshipman at the U.S. Naval Academy at Annapolis. It's called being bricked...as in a brick wall.

The event occurred when a midshipman had a blind date with the sister or the cousin of another classmate for the weekend. The girl would stay at a private home in the town of Annapolis, and the midshipman would come out to meet her on Saturday afternoon.

Typically, they'd start by walking around the town. On Saturday night there'd be a dance. Sunday morning, he'd take her sailing, and by Sunday afternoon, she'd be on her way. If possible, he'd watch her go as he filed back into his own formation.

Sometimes, no matter how gracious a guy would be to this young lady, it was agony. We called such calamities "beasties."

Annapolis is a small town, so reports of a "beastie" started trickling in pretty fast. By Sunday evening, it was pretty obvious who'd had a tough time.

A couple of the ringleaders would get together and discuss it at the Sunday meal: "Oh, that guy really had a real 'beastie' this weekend," and so on. At the end of the meal, the poor man who'd had the worst "beastie" would have to suffer through a bricking ceremony.

His company of about sixty men would assemble in a hallway of Bancroft Hall. Anybody who had any kind of musical instrument would begin to play. Others would chant some kind of jibberish, all in preparation and accompaniment of the "Parade of the Plebes." Typically, the lower classmen (the plebes) would march down the hallway carrying the "duty brick" on a velvet pillow. The leader of the group would present it with an appropriate flourish to the unlucky (and typically embarrassed) partner of the worst "beastie" of the weekend. This is what was called "being bricked."

Fortunately, I lucked out. The brick was never awarded to me. I came very close once. But someone had an even worse "beastie" than I. And that guy was really unlucky, because we didn't have a bricking ceremony the following weekend, and he was stuck with it for two.

I don't think too many women have heard about bricking, as gentlemen would not want to embarrass them. As far as I know, the ceremony started long before I got there, and is still going on.

Ray Sharkey

Known for his unmistakable husky voice, Sharkey has received acclaim for his many acting roles including: *The Idolmaker, Who'll Stop the Rain, Scenes from a Class Struggle in Beverly Hills, The Revenge of Al Capone,* and *Wiseguy.*

I was really a playboy when I met the woman I just married. I mean it got so bad that, let me put it to you this way, when I got up in the morning I'd say, "What do I want today—dark skin, light skin, oriental, fat, thin? What do I do today?"

Each of these chicks, I'd take to one of my routes. That night with my wife, it was the "A" route, which was a walk on the Santa Monica Pier.

I had no intention of ever taking her home that night, but I decided, hey, the moon's great, let me kiss her. I kissed her...next thing I know, it's six in the morning and I'm madly in love! It was a disaster! She had ruined my whole life.

That's what I call a playboy's worst date.

I started perfecting my "playboy technique" as a kid in the tough section of Brooklyn. In those days it was real innocent. It was greaaat! Clubs, Coney Island, picks up girls. Go to Flatbush, find a Jewish girl who would "do it" the first date. Cruise the city.

One summer night, I got in my sports car, a green 1965 TR4A, and drove down to the Village. I stopped smack on the corner of

West 4th and Sheridan Square, right in front of a club called "The Sanctuary," which was a hot place at the time. Go there, pick up "my victims," oh yeah.

I was sixteen. I had on my patchwork boots from Granny's, my cigarette-leg jeans, my silver, silk, shantung shirt. My hair was down to my shoulders and I had an earring on. In those days that was the look.

I'm parked for a light, lookin' real good, when this red Alfa Romeo convertible pulls up alongside me and this really hot chick turns around. Brunette, gorgeous, nice teeth, tight sweater. She smiles real coy, pulls up her blouse and flashes these *great tits*. I mean, she's like begging me, you know. I think, *this* is it! This is *my night*!!!

I say, "Pull over. Park." I'm fumbling, foaming at the mouth. "Pull over, Park! Get in MY CAR!"

I didn't care about privacy. I was doing it RIGHT THERE! IN the car! We're gonna go RIGHT NOW!! Right HERE!!!

She gets in my car, she looks *even* better. She had on a black short skirt (I always loved short skirts), stockings, heels and a tight, angora sweater. Beautiful black hair, big lips, oh, yeah.

She looks at me, very seductive. I put my arm around her. My heart is all the way up to my throat 'cause I'm so ready to do this. She whispers, "Wait a minute...." She slowly hikes up her dress. I'm sixteen, you understand. Imagine the anticipation.

This chick was *a guy*!

Had to be one of the worst moments of my life. It was two in the morning and I was desperate, but I wasn't *that* desperate.

I was pissed! I wasn't pissed that she had tricked me, I was pissed that I wasn't going to score after all that buildup. And what a waste. Those tits were gorgeous; the tits were real. She was a great-looking guy!

I learned my lesson about going to the Village, picking up girls, that's for sure. After that, I started going to Long Island, where middle-class girls loooved "bad boys" like me. And when I was twenty years old, I came to L.A., where I was like a kid in a candy store.

Gail Sheehy

Gail Sheehy is the author of eight books, including *Passages*, *Pathfinders* and *Spirit of Survival*. She is a contributing editor of *Vanity Fair*, and has contributed regularly to *Parade*, the *New York Times Magazine*, *New York Magazine* and other publications.

Every time Tom, my high-spirited Southern boyfriend, would call from the resort on the Jersey shore where he was working as a busboy for the summer, I would hear a noisy party going on. I would be sitting at home in the silence of Wilton, Connecticut, brooding, with Tom's fraternity pin stuck on my boob, signifying to every eligible man that I was unavailable for dates.

Tom had branded me with this fifties symbol of premarital fidelity a couple of weeks before the end of our junior year at the University of Vermont. Since I had no intention of getting married until at least two years out of college, I only consented to the arrangement because I was infatuated with his infectious smile and his true rebel yell.

Tom couldn't afford to come up and see me all summer and I couldn't afford to lose my thrilling job as a bookkeeper at the local department store.

By the next-to-last weekend of the summer, I was so frustrated with my cloistered existence, I jumped at a casual offer made by my neighbor, a gorgeous Yalie, to attend a harmless beach party with a few of his friends.

I went out to the beach party thinking, who would ever know. Just as we were pulling into the driveway laughing and hooting, I heard the squeal of Tom's car farther up the lane. I could tell just from the sound of it that it was he and this was a surprise visit.

I panicked. I took off out of the car, ran into the house, peeling off my sweater as I went (because we'd been drinking beer and we'd gone swimming in our clothes), tore up the stairs and shouted, "Mom, Tom's here! He's coming, I'm covered with sand!" She said, "Don't worry. I'll cover for you."

I jumped into bed, pulled the covers up to my chin so Tom wouldn't be able to see my sandy body, wet clothes and soggy shoes, and prayed my mother would come up with a good excuse.

She came through, I thought. "Oh, Tom, we're so happy to see you, but what a shame you chose this weekend, because Gail's in bed with this terrible flu." Tom took one look at my mother and shouted past her, "I know where you've been and I know who you've been with and that's it!" Then he turned around, got in the car and drove off.

Carelessly, I had dropped my beach bag outside the door on my way into the house. This piece of evidence, along with the sight of the guys leaving my driveway, made him jump to conclusions.

Of course I was upset. But I also thought it was curious that he'd disappeared without a face-to-face argument. Perhaps something else was going on.

Several days later Tom dispelled my anxiety with a contrite telephone call, "Well, I guess I went overboard... and I really do want to see you... so I hope you're gonna come down next weekend as we planned."

I took the train down to the shore. Tom checked me into a room at the hotel where he was working and then announced excitedly "Honey, I want you to meet some new friends of mine. They've invited us for dinner tonight." Which was Friday night of the three-day Labor Day weekend.

We drove his car to a very nicely furnished beach cottage where I was introduced to a stately woman from the Atlanta aristocracy and her daughter Mopsy.

Mopsy looked like a Mopsy.

She was a perfect, little, blonde Chicklet—you know, it pops right out of the wrapper without a blemish—with a snub nose and blue eyes and skin like Naugahyde. I mean, her skin was so smooth, I couldn't see where her eyes fastened in! This made me all the more aware of my plentiful freckles and bookkeeper's pallor.

Mopsy was just the horror you would conjure up if you thought that your boyfriend was going to take up with a beautiful blonde whose most strenuous summer activity was brushing her hair. Thankfully, she wasn't smart. Which didn't seem to matter, since Mother did most of the talking, "It's just been so wonderful having Tom here all summer, because Mopsy was just so lonely. She had nothing to do and he's been such a lovely friend. I've been making all his Southern favorites for him every night. Dinner, everybody?"

I couldn't eat any of the hush puppies, channel fish or black-eyed peas. Naturally, Mother noticed my lack of appetite, but she dismissed it as a typically uncouth and queasy Northern reaction to alien cuisine.

When it was time to go, Tom gave Mopsy a little squeeze that could have been interpreted as an affectionate hug or an insignificant nudge, then whisked me back to my hotel room, where I popped the question, "What does Mopsy mean to you?"

He would be happy to keep both of us, he offered selflessly, then shed a few tears as he tried to make me see what a wretched decision it had been for him. I endured such feeble excuses for two or three hours; I wept, I sobbed, I screamed, and finally I said, "Just go away. I don't ever want to see you again."

He left. Despite my hope that he'd charge back in the door and declare, in his best Southern accent, "I've always been in love with you and there never will be anyone else," he didn't return.

So I stayed in my hotel room for two days and cried.

Subsequently, I realized that he had used the situation to make me feel like I was the guilty one, whereas in reality, he'd probably pinned me in June so he could keep me on ice while he went off to see what else he could find.

His behavior didn't change during our senior year, when Mopsy was back at Sweetbriar and Tom was living in the fraternity house next door to my sorority. Periodically, Tom would stand under my window and let out his rebel yell—a howling which sounded remarkably like a dog in heat. At least, I had the satisfaction of continually refusing his calls.

Ten years later, when Mopsy was divorcing him, he tried again. But the rebel yell was gone.

Now he was a very correct and very boring bank executive. Not a president or a CEO, but a second vice president in a bank in Atlanta, where he was undoubtedly in Mopsy's parents' back pocket.

"I made the wrong choice," he said. This time it was my turn to say no.

Carroll Shelby

Carroll Shelby is, among other things, an auto racing legend, a car designer (Shelby Cobra, Shelby GT 350 Mustang), president of Shelby Industries, a cattle breeder, owner of an African safari company, and creator of Shelby's Original Texas Brand Chili Preparation.

It was a blind date—a sure-fire recipe for disaster if ever there was one. I was about twenty years old and in the Army, going through flight school at Lackland Army Air Base outside of San Antonio, Texas. It was late 1941.

One of the guys in my unit—a kid from Oklahoma we called "Red"—was going out with a really pretty girl, but her folks didn't want them out alone. Probably because he was a soldier. Red asked me if I'd double-date with them so his girl's parents would feel better.

I should have known something was up when Red started describing my date to me—in front of the whole barracks. He said she was terrific looking, had a great personality, and was "hot to trot." I kept thinking that if she was all those things, why didn't Red take her out himself?

Red and his girlfriend picked me up that evening and my date was already in the back of the car. I crawled in and after some brief introductions, off we went. My date wasn't the raving beauty she had been described as being, but she wasn't homely either. We hit it off pretty good. Red brought along some bourbon and a few Cokes and the idea was to drive down by the river and park.

When we got to a desolate spot, Red and his girlfriend got out. They told us to stay in the car while they walked down by the river. That seemed okay to me. They were only gone a few minutes when another car pulled up alongside ours. It was a police car. When I saw that, I got out and went over to the officer. After a quick once-over, he said he was just checking the area, and for me to get back to whatever it was I had been doing. He took off.

What I didn't know was while I was out of the car my date removed her *artificial leg* and propped it up against the door.

I got back in the car and pushed both seats forward so there was more room. The radio was on softly, and the glow from the dial provided a faint light, which was just enough to pick out a few details. My date and I had a couple more pops of bourbon. I was feeling pretty good and my date was beginning to act real friendly. I snuggled up to her and put my hand on her knee.

It was at this point that I noticed her *other knee* was about four feet away!

The effects of the bourbon made my mind begin to spin. What kind of girl was this, I asked myself, who could spread her legs wide enough apart that you could drive a car through them?

Whatever romantic notions I had instantly evaporated. I mumbled something about having to step outside for a minute and when I opened the door something fell out. I didn't see what it was, so I reached down to pick it up, and when I realized what it was, I nearly jumped out of my skin!

At that point, about two dozen guys from the barracks turned on their flashlights and caught me standing there, holding this girl's leg. I was so embarrassed that I dropped it and ran into an open field and hopped a fence. I stopped running and tried to catch my breath and could still hear everyone back at the car laughing and hooting. But I also felt that there was someone else near me. I heard a snort and in the moonlight could make out the dark outline of a bull. A BIG BULL!

I took off running and he followed me. I ran to the middle of the pasture and I think I jumped and caught a limb (of a large oak tree this time!) just as the bull passed under me. I stayed hanging there until the sun came up.

Needless to say, for the rest of flight school, I was continually needled about "getting some leg" and "tearing one off." And that was the last blind date I ever went on.

Bubba Smith

National Football League Hall of Famer Bubba Smith was named All-Pro three times and All-American two times. As an actor, he has appeared in films such as the *Police Academy* series and TV series such as *Semi Tough*.

My oldest brother, Willie Ray, Jr., was probably the best football player I've ever seen, and needless to say, I was his biggest fan. He was a fifth-round draft choice for Kansas City coming out of University of Kansas and I wanted to be just like him.

We'd just moved to this city of 100,000 called Beaumont, Texas, and Willie Ray, Jr., he was the hit of the city! The Big Man on Campus over at the high school. Six-one, one-hundred-ninety pounds, and good looking, too. A real man-child in the ninth grade. I was the little, fat, football player in seventh grade at the junior high school and I was actually in love with this creole-influenced, black girl at my school.

This girl was so gorgeous: in the seventh grade she already looked like a major work. She had the legs of America, as well as olive skin, long, silky, black hair and gray eyes. She's a married woman now and I wouldn't call her name out.

I'd talk to this girl on the phone for hours. You know those two-hour conversations when you talk for thirty minutes and you're quiet for thirty minutes? The phone has started to grow out of your

217

ear? That means you're in love at that age. And each time I'd talk to her, I'd say "Just be cool, and I'll let you say hello to the star." I'm just building and building about my brother, hoping, of course, it'd make her fall for me.

Before I know it, he, my brother, my hero, *he* had taken her out. I didn't have a chance.

I told my mamma, "I'm gonna kill him. I'm gonna wait for him behind these bushes and I'm gonna hit him on the head with this board when he comes around." Imagine how I felt. My hero! He took my sweetheart and I couldn't believe it!

Then he didn't even keep her! And when he finally told me it was over, he said, real macho, "I did it for your own good, man. I knew she wasn't right for you." It took me years to get him back for that. But I did.

It was my junior year at Michigan State and at that time, Michigan State was *mine*. We were undefeated, we were playing for the Big Ten championship, the first stage towards the national championship, and we were *definitely* going to win.

Everyone was fired up. They had about 85,000 people shouting, "Kill, Bubba, Kill." Willie Ray, Jr. came up to see me play, and now, *he* didn't have a chance.

Willie Ray'd been after this girl all day long. She wasn't my girlfriend, but we had gone out and become very good friends, so she would play along with me. I told her, "Just go along with everything he says and around twelve o'clock you tell him you want to go to the ladies' room, and when you go, we'll ease out." This was perfectly planned. I'd spent years thinking about it.

Twelve o'clock came, and she followed the plan to a tee. I met her outside, we snuck off, and went straight to my place and laughed. She told me all the stuff Willie Ray had said:

"Do you know Bubba?" he'd asked.

"Not very well, Willie Ray," she coyly replied, batting her eyelashes. "I met him last week."

"You know how Bubba is, he's a good guy. A prince. A real star." On and on, building and building, just like I was saying about him on the phone back in the seventh grade.

Meanwhile, Willie Ray's running all over this joint looking for his date. He did all those numbers, looking in the bathroom, in the parking lot, with other guys, oh, yeah. But it was over for him, just like it was for me when I introduced him to my creole girl.

Finally, he realized she'd disappeared. But he didn't know *I* was the culprit. I made *sure* he found out.

The first thing he did, he ran up to me and he yelled: "Bubba, I can't believe you'd keep something on me this long!!! I can't believe you still remember that."

"Remember what, Willie Ray?" I asked coolly. (I didn't even bring up the incident.)

"You know, the girl in the seventh grade."

"What girl?"

And then we laughed about it and the game was over.

But a lot of people carry pain like that over into their adult life. When I see it, I say "Whatever it is that's causin' a little coldness, I didn't do it to you. I didn't cause your pain." Like this one, I mean, it was the seventh grade. Everyone gets their heart broken. It's just the process of life.

Ozzie Smith

ODELL MITCHELL, JR.

Shortstop extraordinaire for the St. Louis Cardinals, Ozzie has won ten Golden Glove awards, as well as numerous other distinctions, including Most Valuable Player of the National League championship series.

This wasn't completely a bad date, because through it I met my wife.

It was 1978 and my friend, Dave Winfield, who plays for the Yankees, set me up on a blind date. We'd just got our brains beat out by the Houston Astros, so I was ready to have a good time.

As I was walking out of the Astrodome, a beautiful lady and her girlfriend were waiting, looking out for another ballplayer. They asked me had I'd seen him and so forth. My eyes locked with the beauty, and I guess the rest is history.

I told her I was going out that night on another date but I asked her to give me a call before she went to sleep.

My blind date—she was so unimpressive that I don't remember a whole lot of things about her. We didn't do anything in particular—grabbed a bite to eat, then went to a little club there to do some dancing—but the whole time I kept seeing my future wife in the other girl's eyes and kept wondering whether or not she was going to call.

At about one-thirty or two in the morning, I got lucky. "You told me to call you before I went to sleep," she said. "So I did."

It's too far back to remember whether I had a pleasant dream that night, but I do know I had a *very* pleasant time the next evening on our first date.

We went together long distance for two years, then got married in 1980. Although we didn't win the game the night I met her, I won something even better...her heart.

Frank Snepp

CHIP STONE

After eight years with the CIA, Frank Snepp resigned from the Agency in 1976 to write a book, *Decent Interval,* which criticized U.S. policies and intelligence practices leading up to the evacuation of Saigon. Snepp has taught at the university level and has worked as an investigator for ABC's *20/20* and *World News Tonight.*

I saw first the flouncing blonde hair, then the black silk shirt which clung to this incredible lady like wet tissue paper. She smoked a cigarette as someone might sample a very rare piece of licorice, always in the center of her mouth, her mouth always a bow. She spoke only French. That's what I wanted to refine, my French.

I learned she was born in Tangiers, the illegitimate daughter of a French legionnaire. She had a French marriage, which meant that her husband tolerated her indiscretions. It was 1969.

I had just arrived in Saigon—a novice CIA officer, wide-eyed, twenty-eight years old, and captivated by the exotic Orient and all of its denizens. And here was a round-eye, a blonde round-eye, walking across the street, in downtown Saigon, before the Continental Hotel.

I contrived a meeting at the Cercle Sportif, which was the French sports club in Saigon. It was a wonderful place. The swimming pool was all tiled, blue and rust-colored with plenty of algae; the ladies were all adorned in rubber-band bikinis; and tennis games played by generals and spies from both sides provided constant counterpoint: the thwonk of the tennis balls always discernable at the swimming pool against the thwonk of artillery in the distance.

I wandered up to her at the swimming pool one day—she was in the barest of accoutrements—and asked in my decidedly halting French, "Could you...teach me...a little French? I understand that you're with the école here? And, um, that you handle...French lessons in your spare time?" She was most eager to teach me French.

We sat at a card table at the Cercle Sportif day after day, studying French, under a fan which hung from its spindle like a spider, casting a shadow across the table. I can never forget that constant shadow of the propellor, passing across her face.

After an hour she would always say. "Can't we go and have an aperitif?" We would go downtown, invariably to some of the lower-life bars. She got along very well in those sorts of places. I was very proper, initially, and would never comment when halfway through the aperitif, she would disappear. I was so entranced, I was beguiled. Never in my wildest dreams had I thought I would run into some creature like this in a war zone. She had penetrated my every waking thought.

She also took me to parties. She always knew the strangest people in the French community and the Vietnamese community.

It was she who made the initial come-on, which was done, oh, so casually. One night we were eating shrimp on the top of the Caravelle Hotel. We heard gunfire down below and could see jets streaking in across the river, lobbing fire on somebody, and she said, "Can't we get away from this noise? Can't we get a couple of cigarettes in your room?"

That was the beginning of it. And always in French—which made our communication that much more carnal.

She had a wonderful expression which, to my youthful mind, was like poetry: she would look at the bed with all the rumples and say, "What a wonderful *carte de géographie* we have made," what a wonderful map we have made. As I walked away from these encounters, I remember, always, the smell of Gauloise in my hair and in my clothes.

She talked in her sleep.

At first I couldn't tell what she was saying. Names would sort of float up out of nowhere—Nguyen, Hung, meaningless names. One night I looked at her, sleeping. There was a firefight across the river. Flashes, as if from lightning, flickered across the windowpane. And in that light I saw her arm. There were bruises on it, which was my first warning.

She continued to talk. And as she talked, the names became legion, they became familiar, more significant. Nguyen became Nguyen Cooky and other names. At points, it occurred to me that her familiarity with these names was a little more meaningful than I had thought. But I didn't think quite yet. I had fallen desperately in love with this woman. She carried me away. There was not any point of the compass that I could recognize anymore, she had drawn me in totally.

One night she began murmuring about moving drugs here and there. The next day, I went to CIA files, just on the chance that she might be mentioned. Her name was there as a free-lancer for the Corsicans in Saigon. These people sold information to anyone. And they preyed upon young Americans, generating intelligence from them however they could. We were easy to identify, the CIA. We all drove Fords, we all had the same specially equipped radios, we all dressed in polo shirts with Hong Kong, body-fitted pullovers or campaign jackets, and we all carried forty-fives or Browning automatics. She knew what she was looking for. This was her territory.

I was terrified. I hadn't told her anything, but who knows what that means? You might tell somebody something in a moment of passion or in a moment of indifference that is very important in the larger mosaic. If the CIA had found out that I'd been taken this way, I could have been sent home as a security risk.

So, one night after she'd gone to sleep, after smoking a cigarette laced with something, I left the apartment on Nguyen Hue, went out and bought some of the meanest hash you have ever seen in your life. I came back and I woke her up and I fed it to her.

She began to lose it. Then I used a technique I'd learned in interrogation, the Arabic technique. You strap someone to a chair, mask their eyes, and leave them there hour upon hour. Sensory deprivation takes over. Finally, if it works right, particularly if they're on drugs, they become disoriented. And in this state she told me what she had done.

She was the mistress to a number of high-ranking South Vietnamese officials and she'd performed all sorts of exotic services for them. I had more intelligence on my hands than I knew what to do with, but there was a problem. If I turned this in to the South Vietnamese, they'd throw her in prison and let her rot there. If I didn't report it, I would be betraying everything I was here to do.

At the time there was a prisoner at the National Interrogation Center who would not talk and who was being mistreated by the Vietnamese guards. I decided to arrange a useful little trade off. I gave the guy who was interrogating him the information I'd gathered from her. The South Vietnamese were ecstatic. They thought the prisoner had broken and begun to talk. He wasn't mistreated any more. Then I persuaded this lady to ship out of the country.

I felt betrayed.

I felt betrayed in a fundamental way because in the agency you're conditioned to withhold trust, and when you invest it, it's total. If you're interrogating someone, it's like a love affair. If you have a love affair, it's that one step beyond.

You're not supposed to associate with people who are not American, who have not been cleared. So all of this was terribly risky from the beginning, and all the more dangerous because this lady was totally alien to everything I understood, and totally amoral, in every sense of the word. Yet because of that, she was so sensual, she was so exotic, and sooo dangerous.

Years later she and I rendezvoused in France. I had come out of Vietnam after the collapse and was desperate to find some semblance of everything that had disappeared down the drain in basically a day or so. So I went for her.

I found her in a Communist section of Paris and it was as if I had found a butterfly long divorced from the flowers. The blonde hair had faded. The black tissue shirt had given way to fatigues. There was none of the romanticism that she had brought to the relationship in the beginning. That didn't prevent us from spending the night. With this lady you always spent the night.

And you always walked away from the encounter with the smell of Gauloise in your hair and the satisfaction of knowing, "what a wonderful *carte de géographie* we have made..."

Leigh Steinberg

Leigh Steinberg is a sports attorney/agent to fifty football players, twenty baseball players, an Olympic Gold Medalist figure skater and one professional soccer player.

We had been friendly for some time in the dorms at Berkeley but never dated. I had just broken up with my girlfriend and, on the spur of the moment, I decided to have a date with this blonde, bouncy, young lady on my leisurely drive back home to Los Angeles for summer break. She lived in a very small rural town on the way.

We had a fun day of bike riding in the hot sun. We had a fun day of visiting a park. We had a very nice lunch. And enjoyed each other's company very much.

As soon as we got back to her house, the phone rang. She picked up in the other room, and within seconds I could hear her voice start to be raised.

Moments later, she returned to the living room with a troubled, almost panicked, look on her face. Up to now, this had been an exceptionally cheerful, calm young lady.

"Leigh," she said, "I don't know how to tell you this, but somebody saw us pedaling around town and called my boyfriend."

"Your what?" I tried to cover my total shock.

"Well, you know..." she hedged, "It was a high school romance...But I'm home again, and he's sort of been, like, my boyfriend."

This was certainly news to me. In all of the discussions we had had at Berkeley, she had never alluded to having any other relationships or a boyfriend. But I was the gentleman and said, "Well, okay. I hope this doesn't complicate things for you, but I understand."

"No, you don't understand," she implored. "He's coming over here with a shotgun. And he's talking about shooting you."

"Oh," I gulped.

In a big city, late at night, in an alley, in darkness, many things happen. But it was a very sunny, warm day in the peace-and-love late sixties, and the contrast was incredible. Moreover, there was no one else at home, it was the middle of the afternoon, I was in a tiny town where I'd never been before... Who knows what the mores are?

I tried to stay cool. "Look, obviously if he's coming over here with a gun, I've got to stay here and talk this out with him." (Not a surprising response from a future lawyer.)

"You don't understand," she reiterated, now quite passionately. "*Alone*, I have a chance. *Alone*, I'll be able to defuse him. But if you stay here, the situation will quickly escalate and get out of hand."

"What do you want me to do?"

"Go out the back door, climb over the fence, then work your way back to your car," which was parked a little way down the block.

"You've got to be kidding."

She wasn't.

A beat-up blue "jimmie" pickup screeched into the driveway and out of it stepped this tall, rugged-looking fellow with a gun.

"This is ridiculous!"

"You've got to do this," she said, "Follow me."

After that, I felt like I was in the movie *Deliverance*, as if my actions were happening to someone else: she practically pushed me over the back fence. My pants survived, although I did scrape slightly because I scaled it pretty quickly. I darted through someone else's yard, worked my way back to my car, drove to the first gas station and called her. She whispered reassuringly, "I think it's going to be okay, but it could have been a disaster. I have to go." (Click).

When I got home that night, I called her again. She told me she was simply moritified by her boyfriend's actions, although it didn't stop her from ultimately going back to him.

But passion will do strange things... which very much intensified my strong feelings in favor of gun control.

Gloria Steinem

Co-founder of *Ms.* magazine, Gloria Steinem is one of the country's most widely read and critically acclaimed writers and editors. She also travels as a lecturer and feminist organizer, and appears frequently on television and radio as an interviewer and as a spokeswoman on issues of equality.

© 1987 NBC

There was a well-known psychologist and writer on social relationships—a guy who looked like an ad in the Sears and Roebuck catalogue on his book jackets—who was very persistently asking me out. He sent postcards. He called me. He had other people call and recommend him to me.

It was fairly rare for me to be pursued by a stranger. I tended to meet people through some work setting; we would become friends and then start to go out. But since this man was supposed to be an expert on human relationships, I assumed it wouldn't be much of a disaster.

I never went out to dinner without knowing somebody, so I suggested we meet for lunch at an espresso/cappucino kind of coffee shop on West 56th Street near my apartment. I was living on that block in a one-room studio with another woman, so I used this place as my adjunct office.

He arrived wearing a suit and tie. Mind you, this was the mid-sixties when hardly anybody wore either one. This made him seem old, I suppose, even though he was maybe ten years older than me. The real difference between us was style.

He turned out to be an incredible stuffed shirt. From the moment he arrived he was constricted, self-conscious and full of himself. He talked only about himself.

He told me he had written a book about formerly married people. This formerly married person told me about *his* former marriage, about *his* life history, about *his* other books for general consumption, which all seemed to parallel *his* personal social and emotional history, and *his* other accomplishments. There wasn't a single question, and he clearly felt I should be incredibly impressed.

His whole attitude was that I was very, very, very lucky to have this great expert on positive social interactions paying attention to me, a young, free-lance writer.

This was not my usual experience with writers. But, there's a kind of egocentricity that develops from male narcissism, and it's pretty lethal.

Finally, at about three, I said I had to go to another appointment. He was suddenly put off. He couldn't believe that a woman would leave first—even though it was only lunch. Everything was a one-up game to him. *He* had to make *the first move* toward the exit. The feeling was so vivid, it was as if his beam of human energy abruptly shut off.

I don't think I've been with any man before or since who was so ego-sensitive—and he was telling other people how to have mature relationships!

Part of this behavior was beyond his control, I'm sure. The definition of masculinity is eighty-twenty, or sixty-forty, male to female, so if you propose fifty-fifty, or if you behave fifty-fifty, that's a real threat to some men's identity.

Though this event happened prefeminism, it was one of the common experiences that women had that eventually accumulated into feminism. The whole idea of male authorities as self-importantly dictating relationships—whether through articles or through therapy or through marriage or through dates—was certainly a part of a big iceberg of a problem. It was just the tip of it.

Later on, one of his former wives came to *Ms.* magazine with a thinly disguised article about him in which she revealed that he was a psychologist who had been sleeping with his clients; he had kept a whole cabinet full of files on other women he'd had affairs with. (This was before Phyllis Chesler wrote her book *Women and Madness* and made everyone aware that these encounters were not uncommon.)

We couldn't use the story. The material was far too particular to be of general interest, and it would have been his word against hers if he sued. But I have often thought of the good living we could have made by getting money for *not* printing all of the wild articles that came across my desk, from ex-wives who really knew the truth, however difficult to prove, about well-known men.

As a result of this encounter, I would highly recommend having lunch with a man before you consider going out with him. And talking to his ex-wives and ex-friends before marrying him.

Jake Steinfeld

Jake Steinfeld is the "Fitness Trainer to the Stars," as well as executive producer and star of the TV series *Body by Jake*.

I was one of the hosts of a Muscular Dystrophy Telethon. You answer the phones. The M.C. walks around and introduces everybody—introduces Jake, "Body by Jake Steinfeld." (You know the score.) Pretty soon, I start getting personal phone calls, which is not something you're supposed to get on a telethon. These women call up, "How ya doing? I just saw you on TV. I'd like to go to bed with you."

"Thank you very much, ma'am. How much are you pledging?" (Click.)

This one woman with a really sexy voice kept on calling back and begging to meet me.

"Look," I told her, "I'm on television. I can't have this conversation with you."

"Please," she teased.

"Call me later." (Click.)

Seven minutes later she calls back and I say, "Holy shit."

Now, I was always one for a beautiful woman, 'cause I'm like any regular guy, I love a beautiful woman. So I say, "What do you look like?" (Remember, this is on television.) She goes, "I'm a tall, blonde, blue-eyed model. Very wealthy." Now, I'm a Brooklyn guy, and the second you say "blonde, blue-eyed" to me, it's a done deal. "Okay" I say, just as the M.C. comes around again and I make

233

believe that I'm writing down her pledge, "How much are you donating, Miss? Yes, of course. And what's your phone number?"

I never wanted to go on a blind date because I always heard horror stories, but this girl sounded like a zillion bucks, so I decided to go through with it.

I make a reservation for Saturday night (the one night of the week when I relax, have a slow dinner) at my favorite Italian restaurant in Beverly Hills, La Famiglia. Even before I was anybody, I'd walk in there and they'd say, "Jake, how ya doing, Jake?", so whoever I took in there thought I was a big shot.

I'm all psyched up. I'm dressed. Washed the car. The whole program. Figuring this is IT. I'm going to get married from a phone call on a telethon!

I told her to meet me in front of Gucci's (you want to talk about schmuckiness on my part), 'cause I'm cool. I figure let me drive by first, check her out from a distance, because I'm expecting the most unbelievable lady in the universe.

Now, I'm no Robert Redford, okay, but when I drive by Gucci, I see this girl who, regretfully speaking, is nothing like the lady she said was on the phone. She was short. She was heavy. There was nothing about her that was attractive. Wish I could say she had gorgeous brown hair. But no. She had frizzy hair. I'm going to myself, "Get out of here now!" But I come from a Jewish family with a lot of Jewish guilt and the other side of me says, "You can't just leave this person hanging. That's rude. Not cool. Not mature. Park the car and meet her at Gucci."

We walk in the front door of La Famiglia and Joe, the guy who runs the place, greets me by name. We shake hands. "How ya doing, Joe? I got my... um... *cc-cousin* with me. I have to keep *an eye* on her tonight. (Wink, wink.) Can you just give me something *by the door* so we can just eat and cruise real fast?" He gives me this look like, I hope this is your cousin, because he's seen me with some really nice-looking, bright women. I love bright women! That's the thing that turns me on the most. And here I am with this—what I thought was a woman, who turns out to be a twenty-two-year-old girl—and she's literally a monster.

We sit down and we having nothing to say to each other, even though prior to this evening, we've had at least half a dozen long conversations about everything—life, sex, everything—and she was great.

I ordered scallops, which is the littlest thing on the menu, so that I can just drink 'em down. Done. We finish dinner, I don't even get dessert, and she says, "Jake, I have to ask you a question."

"What?" (Am I paying the check?)

"Can you drive me home?"

"What do you mean? Where's your car?"

"Well... my mom dropped me off."

"Your *mom* dropped you off!?"

Before, I was a good guy, now I'm mad!

We drive to this palatial mansion in Brentwood. No kidding around: there were two Rolls Royces, the guard opens the gate, the works. I'm going, "Wait a second. What's going on here?"

"Please come in," she says. "My mom wants to meet you."

It's eleven o'clock at night and her mom answers the door in this halter top and hot pants. "Come in, come in," she says.

Now, at the time I was doing *The Hulk* at the Universal Studio Tours and I was very crazy. Very crazy. I was into everything and anything just to have a good time.

I go inside, sit down on the couch, and the mom says to the daughter, "Why don't you go up and get your photo album to show Jake? I'll get him some coffee." I protest, "No, no, no. I don't drink coffee. I don't like pictures. I have to get up early." I'm trying everything. (Usually I'm great at leaving, but nothing here is working.)

The daughter goes running up the stairs and the mother disappears into the kitchen to get the coffee... Comes out *naked*. The MOM is *NAKED!*

Remember what Buckwheat looked like when he got scared: his hair would stand straight up and his eyes would bug out? That's how I looked, I'm sure. Because up until then, I thought I was pretty hip, but when she walked out naked, it was like—Mrs. Robinson!!!

I stuttered, "Um...um...I-I-I got a-a girlfriend and I-I c-can't do this!"

"Relax. My daughter isn't coming down for the rest of the evening."

All I can recall running through my mind was GET OUT OF THAT HOUSE! They're probably going to kill you after this! Which is irrational, because I'm a big guy. But when something like that happens, you're totally shocked.

I can't remember what she looked like, because I was looking right through her. All I remember is the naked body of this fifty-year-old woman standing in front of me saying soothingly, "You're probably nervous. You have our phone number. Call us any time."

With that, I stood up, ran out, and never went on a *blind date* or a *telethon* again.

H. N. Swanson

H. N. Swanson co-founded and edited the magazine *College Humor.* He has been an agent for writers such as Cornell Woolrich, F. Scott Fitzgerald, Raymond Chandler, and, currently, Elmore Leonard.

When I was editing *College Humor* in Chicago, one of several campus magazines around the country meant to brighten the day, I bought a story from Adela Rodgers-St. John. Adela was a feature writer whose stories were in the papers often and she was married to Dick Hyland, a big football star at Stanford. Together they wrote a football novel which I serialized in my magazine.

Well, that novel got a lot of attention in Hollywood, so when I came out to the West Coast for my yearly visit, Adela invited me to one of her swank parties.

"I've got a date for you," she told me.

I said, "Whatever you say, kid. I'm in your hands."

Well, she had a driver pick me up at the Ambassador Hotel to take me to Adela's ranch in the suburbs. In the thirties, anyone who had a place a little bit out of town called it a ranch; it sounded good.

When I got there, Adela led me out on the terrace, introduced me all around, and took me to my date. "Swanie, I'd like to introduce you to Clara Bow."

Clara at the time was the hottest chick in creation. Paramount's star. The IT girl. I didn't know that much about her but I was impressed with her curves. Even her curves had curves. I can't spell out all of her glory, but she had a hell of a body. That night she was sporting something with a lot of fringes. It was a skimpy little number, boy.

"I have a confession to make," Clara told me. "I came here with a date."

"Who is he?"

She told me he was the swimming champ from Finland and he was out here collecting all kinds of awards. She tried to make me feel easier, "I don't want to be with the guy, but I got set up by the studio."

Well, Hoagy Carmichael's "Stardust" started to play. We had a couple of dances and sat down at a table before the big Finnish swimmer noticed his date was missing and came over to us. I don't know if he was an Olympic star, but he was the best they had to offer in Finland. At the moment, the best was roaring drunk. He was abusive as all hell to Clara, and I tried to settle him down. "Sit down and have a drink," I said.

"Drink? Smell my breath and have yourself a drink."

"I hear you're a swimming star," I said. "How about a demonstration?"

He thought that was a good idea. So he stripped off his jacket, and beneath it all he actually had a swimsuit. He was ready to go.

He dove into the pool with a grand splash and then sank like a stone. Two guys in spiffy clothes went after him with a rake and finally got him out onto dry land, where he was spouting water like a whale.

That left me with Clara. She confided in me that she was annoyed with all these nuisance dates. Big celebrities with big egos.

I don't remember if I kissed her, but I'm sure I did. We all kissed everyone in those days.

Andrew Tribe

As a music producer, Andrew Tribe has worked with bands such as Deep Purple. For film, he co-produced *The Pirates of Penzance.*

I met a very beautiful woman and decided I was heavily in lust. She arranged to meet me at a restaurant in Woodland Hills. I had no idea where Woodland Hills was at the time. I was visiting from London and was staying far out in the boondocks of the San Fernando Valley.

I park my car outside the restaurant and go in. I'm wearing light-colored cotton trousers and a white jacket. We have this fairly ordinary meal. About twenty minutes after we've eaten the food, we're having a very animated discussion—all my usual boring stories and anecdotes—and I start to get these desperately sharp pains in my chest and stomach.

Now, at the time I was having trouble with what's called a hiatus hernia, so I was aware of these things happening. But these pains were getting worse and worse. I mean real shooting, darting pains. So I jokingly say to her, "I think I'm having a heart attack."

She starts laughing. "Do you normally act like this?"

"Only when I look at women like you...," I flirt as the pains start to subside.

We're getting on quite well, and I'd like to bore her a little longer, but this restaurant is really out to lunch, so I say, "Is there somewhere else we can go and talk?" She says, "There's a place nearby. Come with me. It's only around the corner, but you won't find it."

We get in her car, which is a white VW convertible with white upholstery and drive around to this other "typical-Valley-awful" place called "Thank God It's Friday." It's pick-up city in there, with an endless bar down the middle. We order drinks, and within seconds the pains start back up. Once again, I didn't say anything, I just carried on talking. Unfortunately, these pains are getting worse and worse and worse, I'm now sweating, and finally I have to say, "Excuse me, I've just got to go to the bathroom."

I go to the bathroom, come back, sit down, and about two minutes later I get this gigantic pain again. So sharp, I'm having difficulty even sitting up straight.

How can I put this delicately to you? I *thought* that it was *gas.* So I thought if I just let this pass very quietly, I'll be okay... And then there's this *horrendous explosion* in my pants! Meanwhile, I'm carrying on talking to her like nothing has happened, but I'm wishing I could die, very quickly, on the spot, because I'm now deeply in love, you understand. I'm deep in love.

At the same time I'm thinking, What the hell am I going to do now? I've only been back from the bathroom no more than two or three minutes. So I start feeling around in my pockets and say, "I think I left my lighter in the toilet." Why I didn't say I have to go make a phone call or something I don't know.

Then I have to get up. Remember, I've got light pants on and a white jacket. And I *know* it's going to be horrendous. I can't see it, but I'm soaking wet. On top of everything else, everything's sticking to me, and I see I'm going to have to walk past that long, long bar full of perfect-looking Valley girls and guys.

I decide to walk completely the wrong way round so my date won't be able to see my best side. "I'll just take a little gander as I go," I say. She looks at me like, strange guy. First he's having a heart attack. Then he's sweating. Now he's walking the wrong way to the restroom.

The walk to the restroom feels like three miles. Inside, I find forty-five guys, all combing their hair. There's only one cubicle, it's got no lock on it and a tiny, little swinging door. In other words, there's no privacy at all and I've got to go in for a major cleaning-up operation!

So, I stand there for twenty-five minutes waiting for the restroom to empty out. Of course, it doesn't, because it's the busiest time of the night. It's about eleven, eleven-thirty. People are going in and out. It's like a railway station! In the meantime, I have another attack, while I'm standing there.

I wanted to run away, but I didn't know where my car was because out here in California *everything looks the same!* Then I thought, if I do "a runner," I'll blow it with this girl, and she's a friend of a friend of mine in England; the story will go right back to everyone and I'll look like a complete idiot. Maybe I should call somebody? Who can I phone? I don't have my phone book. It's in my car. I can't go buy new clothes and throw these away. I can't have a shower. I can't do anything!

Meanwhile, I'm having another attack.

By now, this has gone on for about forty minutes and I'm in a terrible state. I'm sweating. I'm panicked. Even more so when I see the damage. It was totally unspeakable. Put it this way, I was humming very loudly and smelled like a very bad deodorant. On top of that, I'd left this very attractive girl sitting alone at a table at a singles bar. She must have thought I'd gone because I couldn't have spent *all this time* looking for my lighter in the toilet!

But there's always a way out, I thought. I'm just going to try and bluff this through.

I go back to the table and she smiles sweetly. Doesn't say anything, as American girls do. I say, "I'm terribly sorry, I just remembered I had to make a phone call. It took much longer than I anticipated."

"Where did you call?"

"London."

"London?" she utters with surprise.

"I called collect," I reply nonchalantly.

"Oh."

I sit down again, praying that the door's not going to open and send my fragrance downwind, and she says, "I've got to go now. I've got to be up early in the morning."

"That's fine. Just tell me where the car is, I think I'll get some air." (I didn't want her to know I was feeling bad because, again, that would look silly.)

"No, no, it's too far away. I'll drop you off."

Unfortunately, you recall, her *white* convertible had *white* upholstery. "We English love fresh air. If you could just put the top down...."

I get into the car and I'm trying *not to sit* on the white seat, but still *look like I'm sitting;* I've got my hand on the back of her seat. I've got my elbow on the back of my seat. I've got my forearm along the door and on the dash. Dudley Moore could have done this perfectly in *"10"*. Meanwhile, she's going 100 miles an hour, throwing me around the corners, and I'm hanging on for dear life, with the top down, being blown to pieces.

We reach my car, which is a loaner from a friend, and also has *white* upholstery, and I don't know how I'm going to get out of her car without soiling her white seat and *not letting on* that I'm *not sitting*. So, I point behind her and ask, "What's that place over there? She looks the other way and I quickly dive out.

She turns back, "What?"

"The one over there," I say, indicating a really ordinary looking building.

We have this stupid conversation about bland architecture and I think I'm safe because I've now got my back out of the car and she can only see me from the waist up. That sense of false security quickly vanishes when she decides to put the hood back up and trots round behind me. I don't know if she notices the damage because she kisses me goodbye and says, "I'll see you again."

I bet you won't.

At the very back of mind, all the time, I wanted to burst out laughing.

I get into my friend's white car, and as I slip into the seat, the relief of it... It happens again and I don't care.

I drive back to my friend's house, and thank God, no one was there. Except for their white shitsu dog, who was very pleased to see me.

I saw the girl again for about two months. She never said a word. American girls are like that, you know.

John Van Hamersveld

John Van Hamersveld has designed hundreds of album covers and rock posters, including the Beatles' *Magical Mystery Tour* and the Rolling Stones' *Exile on Main Street*, sportswear for Jimmy Z's, murals for the L.A. Olympics, and *The Endless Summer* poster.

HONYEA THOMPSON/1968

I'd just completed the new album cover for the Jefferson Airplane, which was an atomic bomb theme called the *Crown of Creation*, and I was very rock-'n'-rolled out: I had my Kent cigarettes and my black velvet pants and my white Italian vinyl shoes and my Day-Glo socks and my white silk shirts. My hair was to my shoulders and I had a cowboy hat which was custom-made in Texas.

I'd been living with a woman for about three years when her mother died, and after that we decided that it was over. Little did I know that she was a millionairess whose mother gave her an oil well after my relationship with her ended, even though I had put her through art school.

Somewhat disillusioned, I got on a plane and I went to London to see the Beatles. We knew each other because I had designed a cover for them as well as for a lot of other bands such as the

Grateful Dead, the Airplane, and the Blue Oyster Cult. Derek
Taylor, who worked with the Beatles, fixed up my English working
papers, and I was hanging out with Alan Aldridge, the artist at the
time who was creating songbooks with the Beatles.

Every evening during the six months I was there, I would go
over to these two brothers' underground flat where my friends
from San Francisco, Stanley Mouse and Bob Seideman, were
staying. One of the brothers went to St. Martins, which was the
big art school where all the bands would play and everyone was
discovered. The second brother was a photographer whose claim
to fame was the most recent Who album cover for *Tommy*.

Their place was literally in a cavity underneath a building and
in the evening, it became a very hip dope den. The scene. All this
hash was being smoked and all these rock-'n'-roll people were
dropping by. We'd be standing there with Eric Clapton or
someone from Pink Floyd or the manager for Small Faces or
whatever men were of importance in that scene at that time.

And in the background there were always these girls, these
beautiful English girls. As an outsider, you didn't know quite what
the deal was. You assumed they had boyfriends who were there in
the center of things, but you could never be sure.

As these nights went on, I kept seeing these beautiful eyes
flirting with me. They belonged to Christine—a dark-haired,
French-looking, English girl who was very sleek, like a black cat.
Christine was about twenty-one and was not quite a model. That
meant she was living the life of a groupie and chasing photographers who were in the "glam" scene. The rock world is sort of
dark and satanic compared to the world of a model, and its women,
in many cases, are more aggressive than the men.

One night, as we were going out the door in a confused state,
Christine took me by the hand and said, "Here, why don't you
drive me home? I can't drive this car, I borrowed someone's
Citroën." From the moment she touched me, it was obvious what
was going to happen.

I drove the European Citroën over to her apartment, which was part of a group of rooms with a loo at the end of the hall, that belonged to the Who. In England, at that time, the economy was such that everybody grouped up in these flats.

Christine's room was painted red. It had big rococo mirrors that leaned against the wall and went from floor to ceiling. And velvet. Lots of black velvet and red velvet curtains and persian rugs. The perfect environment for a slick feline.

I had this wonderful evening and, at about five o'clock in the morning, I woke up, hopped in my clothes and took the tube back over to my apartment and fell asleep. Maybe half the day went by, then I zipped over to meet Seideman and Stanley Mouse at the underground flat, before going off to lunch or tea or some event, as we did every day.

I knocked on the flat door, it opened, and there was the photographer. "You poked my bird, bloke."

I didn't know what to say. I wasn't sure if I was being set up for a fight, although I knew I could win because was a foot taller and tougher.

I just said, "Well, um, you know, it's your relationship. I thought you understood what it was." He probably didn't know what I meant by that comment. To me it pointed up what I learned about Englishmen: that they are so arrogant about keeping this clubby atmosphere going, which their often amazing women can't break into, that their women all go off and find other relationships, particularly with men from other countries.

Later that evening, Christine appeared at my apartment and begged for forgiveness. "I didn't mean to tell him . . . ."

I've always thought that this encounter with Christine was a bit like an eddy off a river. I think we both wanted to continue, but she blew the whole thing by telling him. Now, why she made that decision, I'll never know.

Maggie Wagner

DON ADAMS

Maggie Wagner is an actress living and working in New York and California. She has appeared in several feature films, including *Anna* with Sally Kirkland, *White Hot* with Robby Benson, and *Working Girl.*

Maggie Wagner and Sally Kirkland in "Anna"

It was about twenty minutes into the Trinity High School prom and I *had* to dance with our French teacher, Monsieur Bolluc. God knows why. I had an absolutely adorable date, the son of "Trixie" from *The Honeymooners,* and I preferred a man who was sixty-seven years old, and had been in and out of the hospital that year for an eye problem.

Monsieur Bolluc was short. He was bald. He was very French. No matter what the weather, he always dressed so well in quality, beautifully tailored suits. And he always wore his little round glasses. Quite often, he would invite us to his house for little tea parties. And he loved my big brown eyes.

He was a really special person—so ebullient, so huggable...and a very hard French teacher.

I don't know why I had to dance with him. But I had this thing. Maybe it was the room.

It, too, was very French. Very lush. Burgundy colored. Chandeliers, mirrors. You know it, Regine's? Not the restaurant, the room upstairs.

It was 1978, the height of the disco phase. Donna Summer and the heavy beat. Why I thought a sixty-seven-year-old man, who

247

reminded me of my recently deceased grandfather, would want to dance to this loud, hot music, I don't know.

I went up to him and said, "Oh, please, dance with me, Monsieur Bolluc."

"No, Maggie," he said in his little French accent.

I came back again.

"Not this song."

So I waited. "Macho Man" started to play. I tried once more, "Now?"

"Okay, now... But not a long time."

We started dancing. I'm singing along, "Macho, Macho Man. I want to be a Macho Man." Everything was fine. And the next thing I know, he held his heart and collapsed at my feet, right there in the middle of the dance floor.

I knew he was dead. He just didn't look alive anymore. "Help!" I was screaming, in time to "Macho, Macho Man!"

Everything stopped. The music stopped. And then I realized: I encouraged this man to dance with me, I probably killed him.

We all rushed outside and the headmaster said, "I'm sorry to announce that Monsieur Bolluc has passed away. Everyone gasped, "Oh, my god!" then looked straight at ME!

It was the worst thing in the world. I don't think anyone really thought it was my fault, but by the time I got home to my mother, I was crying hysterically.

She gave me a Valium. I was seventeen. She said, "Take a Valium." That started my drug habit. (I'm just kidding.)

People said to me, "This was bound to happen. He was sick. He must have had a heart condition, not an eye problem. It wasn't your dancing." But I'm sure if he had stayed home and slept, he probably wouldn't have died that night.

I've gone down in the annals of Trinity High School history, because, to this day, when people meet me they say, "Aren't you Maggie? The one who killed Monsieur Bolluc!"

It's so horrifying that it's funny. It's like theater of the absurd. It's absolutely crazy that it happened at a prom for one of the richest, preppiest, Episcopalian high schools in New York City, and even crazier that, in college, I became a French major.

Arnetia Walker

Actress and singer Arnetia Walker has appeared on Broadway, off Broadway, in film, and television, with roles in *Dreamgirls, Scenes from a Class Struggle in Beverly Hills, The Sign in Sydney Brustein's Window,* and *Two Gentlemen of Verona* for Joseph Papp.

I'm not going to name names. This was a basketball player in New York, and if I'm not mistaken, he plays with the Knicks.

I was doing *Dreamgirls* on Broadway and the three of us, me, Sheryl Lee Ralph, and I believe, a girl, Linda Loy, were asked to do a benefit as the Dreamgirls at Studio 54. We sang a couple of songs from the show, and then this guy from the Knicks came up to me and was very persistent about me going out with him.

I'm not really into basketball players. I really don't even know that much about the sport, or any sport. Most of the time, when I meet these guys, other people are all excited, "Oh, that's so and so." I'm like, "Oh, yeah?" "Yeah." Just tall.

Every day for about two or three weeks, this Knick would show up at the stage door at eleven P.M., when the show lets out, or call me, or send me flowers. Every night!

One evening I found him out there in the snow, waiting. I mean, it was a blizzard almost. I felt so sorry, I thought, "Well, let me go to dinner with this guy."

He wasn't a great conversationalist. He wasn't the most well-read person in the world. But he was nice, I guess.

After dinner he took me home. As we pulled up to my place he looked at his watch and he said, "One o'clock, oh, wow! My most favorite show in the whole world is coming on right now."

I said, "What's that?"

He said, "*Star Trek*. Can I please come up to your house and watch it? Because if I go home now I'm going to miss the first half of it."

I was like, "Well, yeah, okay, all right—come on up."

When we got in the door I had to, you know, use the bathroom, so I told him, "Please, make yourself at home and I'll be back in a few minutes."

Well, when I came back he was lying up in my living room without a stitch of clothes on!

I demanded, "What are you doing?"

He said innocently, "Well you told me to 'make myself at home' and this is how I watch *Star Trek* at home." I said, "Get Out! Get your clothes and GET OUT!!"

I could have thrown him out with his clothes in his hands, but I let him get dressed. It was cold outside, I'm not heartless!

Next day he called and was a little upset with me. He just couldn't understand, *really couldn't understand*, what he had done to disturb me. I said, "If you don't understand, then we really should just stop this right here, 'cause I don't think we have very much in common!" (I mean it's funny now, but it wasn't funny then. It was like, the *nerve* of you!)

Now I hardly remember what he looked like. He wasn't unattractive. He wasn't threatening. It's just the greatest impression he left on me was lying up in my living room, stark naked.

Neil Walsh

Former New York City commissioner for public events and civic affairs, Walsh is now the CEO of one of the largest privately owned insurance organizations in the nation.

I was at a party and I met an absolutely beautiful blue-eyed blonde. I must say, there is one thing in the world that really gets my adrenalin going, and that's a beautiful, blue-eyed blonde. We got into a conversation. "I'd like to get together and have dinner." She said she'd be delighted and gave me her number.

I wrote the number down. But when I wrote it down, I spilled something on it, so I couldn't read the number straight. She told me that she lived in the east seventies. I looked in the New York City directory and there, in the east seventies, was a girl with the exact same name.

I called her up. "This is Neil Walsh. Can you make dinner on Wednesday night? I have some dear friends of mine who are coming in from London, Lord and Lady Benson Churchill, we'll go to '21.'"

"Love to," she said.

My driver pulled my car up to her apartment. I buzzed the buzzer. She let me up. Went upstairs. Pushed the bell. Opened the door. There was somebody that resembled a tall, blue-eyed blonde as much as a...I can't tell you—It was an absolutely, completely, different person!

251

She must have weighed over three-hundred pounds. She was sloppy. The apartment was an absolute disaster. The dirtiest place I've ever seen in my life. (Is there any chance I had a lobotomy?)

My first thought was, I'm double-parked. I'll meet you downstairs. But before I could say anything, she put her coat on and walked out the door to go to "21" with my fancy friends, Lord and Lady Benson Churchill.

As we rode down the elevator, I just didn't know what in the world to do, and as we emerged from the building, my driver, Mr. Charles, who's been with me about twenty years, and knows me well, knew that *this* woman was not my type. Someplace, somewhere, there had to have been either a mistake or a gross misunderstanding.

We got into the backseat, drove a few blocks, then my driver made the sound of a ring, picked up the phone in the car and said dramatically, "Oh, my heavens! He's right in the car." He hands me the phone and says, "Aw, there's a big emergency!" and I begin an almost Academy Award–winning performance.

I say breathlessly, "No. What happened? You're kidding! Was anybody killed? Thank God! I was on my way to dinner, but I'll cancel. I have some people—I'm sure they'll understand—I'll go straight to the airport and fly to Columbus."

I make out like I'm hanging up the dead phone and I dial TWA, "What time is your next plane to Columbus?" *They say* there are none until the next morning and *I say,* "Nine-fifteen tonight? Perfect. I'll take it!"

I hang up and turn to the lady, "A client of mine has had an explosion in his factory and there is a tremendous amount of damage. I will have to leave for Columbus immediately. I'm very sorry. Can I take a raincheck on this?"

Needless to say, I ripped up that raincheck.

Carole Markin

STEVEN ARNOLD

Over the past few years Carole Markin has worked as a filmmaker, costume designer, writer, director, producer, designer, public television executive, board president, and artist.

I figured I probably should forget it when I found a half-written love note to a girl named Lizzie on the first page of his journal. He'd dropped it on the floor after film class. I returned the notebook without a word, but it certainly didn't diminish my crush.

He had everything nobody else did in Cambridge—sex, health, and the accent of suspenders. A live Californian in a dead, ivory tower. Or so it seemed to me at least. He had a great body from years of sailing, wild curly hair, a neatly trimmed beard, and riveting blue eyes.

I told my roommates if nothing happened before Thanksgiving, I'd settle for a preppy and give up. But somehow, in late November, I got him to ask me to the movies at the most unromantic time of the week, Sunday afternoon. We met in front of the theater, both of us bundled up for an early Boston winter.

As we walked inside, the trailers were playing, so our eyes had to adjust as we found seats in an empty row. The theater wasn't too filled for this German movie. I noticed a single girl in front of us, also settling in for the show.

After we peeled off our coats, he asked if I'd like to share some popcorn. I said sure. So he slipped out to get us some.

When he returned, he sat down next to the other single girl, in the other empty row, in the otherwise empty show.

Granted, I had put my feet up on the seat in front of me, making me look a bit like a snail from the back, but I was more than devastated. I thought, he doesn't even know what I look like, how could I have a chance?

In fact, he didn't even notice his mistake until he leaned over and offered the stranger a handful of corn.

With an awkward apology about being blind without his glasses, he took his appropriate seat next to mine. I forgave him for his silly mistake, but I couldn't forgive myself for being so boring and undistinctive that I made no impression on a guy in my film class of ten.

When I told my roommates about this incident, they said I *definitely* should forget it.

Unfortunately my hormones couldn't. In fact, my lust grew worse by the day. I'd been having a series of terrible dates and limp one-night stands, so I was desperate for something daring and different and talented and trouble.

But I'm a persistent person, I guess, and decided to change my own chemical deadline. If nothing happened before Christmas, I vowed, I *really* would forget him.

Sometime in December, we wound up in a tiny editing room viewing a cut of a short film I'd directed that term, a stirring documentary about the Harvard Police Department. And somehow, amid comments about camera angles and jump cuts, we wound up in a very hot embrace. If twenty people didn't have the key to that room, we might have found ourselves rolling among strips of film on the tile floor. Instead, I pulled myself away from his compelling lips and said, "So, when are we going to...?"

He smiled mischeviously and suggested now.

I smiled mischeviously and looked at my watch. "I hate to tell you this," I said between teasing kisses, "I'm having dinner with another guy."

"When?" he asked rather coyly but still stunned.

"Now," I replied softly, fondling his backside.

He wanted to withdraw but the mutual passion was a little too intense.

"It's just a dinner," I said, "but I could come by your room at 8:30...?"

He thought that sounded like a good idea.

I separated myself from him with great difficulty and went off to my dinner with quite a glow.

At 8:30, I promptly appeared at his door. By 8:35, we were already in bed. At ten, I looked at my watch.

"I hate to tell you this," I said.

"What?"

"I have to go to a meeting."

"When?"

"Now."

This time he fondled my backside and shoved me back under the covers.

"I'm organizing something in the dorm that I can't get out of. But you could come by my dorm at midnight?"

He thought that sounded like a good idea.

At 12:00, he appeared at my door. By 12:10, we were back in bed.

My roommates didn't know any of this had happened. I'm really quite private when it comes to my bed.

Right in the middle of making love, all of a sudden the fire bell rang. He thought we should burn in the heat of passion. I thought that sounded like a good idea.

We decided we were having too much fun to die and forced ourselves into our clothes and out to the courtyard. What could be worse than being exposed to the public scrutiny of three-hundred gossipy members of a co-ed dorm before you reach a climax?

I figured he'd never touch me again. My insecurity proved to be as false as the fire alarm, because he became my boyfriend for the better part of two and a half years.

How Bad Was *Your* Date?

If you think *your* Worst Night Out really was the ultimate "date from hell," please send it in. You might just win a FREE VACATION, compliments of Citadel Press/Carol Publishing Group.

We will award a four-day/three-night stay in a Doral Hotel (Miami or Manhattan)—airfare included—to the storyteller (and guest) who submits the best tale of romantic woe to our top panel of judges, including the publisher and the author.

For style, follow the format established in this book. Be honest and outrageous! Should there be a future edition of *Bad Dates* published by our company, the "Best of the Worst" will be included.

Note: All entries must be postmarked no later than September 30, 1990; and no entries will be returned.

Submit entries to: Bad Dates Contest, Citadel Press/Carol Publishing Group, 600 Madison Avenue, New York, NY 10022.